Jan/2021

SURPRISING SPIES

NOOR INAYAT KHAN, Sufi princess spy, playing the *vina*
(a stringed instrument from India) in
The Hague, Netherlands, 1937

SURPRISING SPIES

UNEXPECTED HEROES OF WORLD WAR II

KAREN GRAY RUELLE

HOLIDAY HOUSE · NEW YORK

Dedicated to unexpected heroes everywhere, with gratitude.

Library of Congress Cataloging-in-Publication Data
Names: Ruelle, Karen Gray, author.
Title: Surprising spies : unexpected heroes of World War II / Karen Gray Ruelle.
Description: First edition. | New York : Holiday House, 2020
Summary: "Seven Allied spies of World War II who fooled the Nazis
are profiled in this book, including a Sufi princess, a major-league
baseball player, a magician, and others"—Provided by publisher.
Includes bibliographical references and index. | Audience: Ages 8–12
Identifiers: LCCN 2017023913 | ISBN 9780823437573 (hardcover)
Subjects: LCSH: World War, 1939–1945—Secret service—Juvenile literature.
Espionage—History—20th century—Juvenile literature.
Spies—Biography—Juvenile literature. | Women spies—Biography—Juvenile literature.
Classification: LCC D810.S7 R774 2018 | DDC 940.54/860922—dc23
LC record available at https://lccn.loc.gov/2017023913

CONTENTS

Germany and Italy were two of the
three major powers that formed the
Axis alliance.

NORWAY FINLAND

SWEDEN

DENMARK

IRELAND UNITED
KINGDOM NETH. SOVIET UNION

BELG. GERMANY POLAND

CZECHO-SLOVAKIA

HUNGARY

FRANCE SWITZ. ROMANIA

YUGOSLAVIA

ITALY BULGARIA

PORTUGAL SPAIN TURKEY

GREECE

INTRODUCTION

IT WAS 1933, and Germany's economy was in bad shape. Factories were closing and people across the country were living in poverty, desperate for jobs and food. At that time, Germany's chancellor, Adolf Hitler, was head of the Nazionalsozialistische Deutsche Arbeiterpartei—the National Socialist German Workers' Party, or Nazi party. His ideas about what was wrong with the country especially appealed to these Germans who were living in such poor conditions.

Hitler used persuasive speeches to blame Jewish people for Germany's troubles, and because there was already a lot of anti-Semitism (hatred for Jews) in the country, it wasn't difficult for Hitler's supporters to accept what he told them: that Jews were responsible for the problems in the world, and they had to be destroyed.

The following year, upon the death of Germany's president, Hitler proclaimed himself the *führer*—the supreme leader—of Germany. He promised to make Germany great again. But his ultimate goal went beyond lifting the country out of economic depression. He wished to conquer all of Europe, and perhaps the rest of the world, too.

The Nazis especially hated Jews, but they also hated anyone else who didn't fit into the Aryan stereotype. People who were considered Aryan had physical features that were typical of many northern Europeans, including blond hair and blue eyes. They were, in Hitler's words, "pure" and free of Jewish influence. Those who didn't fit the Nazis' ideal mold also included Slavs, Romani people, Jehovah's Witnesses, people who were not heterosexual, people who were not cisgender, the mentally ill, and people with physical differences or disabilities. Hitler wanted to destroy them all.

BENITO MUSSOLINI, prime minister of Italy, and **ADOLF HITLER** during an official visit to what was then occupied Yugoslavia in the early 1940s

Italy's prime minister, Benito Mussolini, was in league with Hitler. Like Hitler, he was a fascist—a dictator with complete power over everything in their country, who doesn't allow anyone to disagree with them. While Hitler focused on conquering his neighbors in northern and central Europe, Mussolini sent the Italian army into the nations surrounding the Mediterranean and into North Africa, where he hoped to rule.

Around the same time, Japan's Emperor Hirohito planned to vanquish all of Asia. In 1937, the Japanese army invaded China and continued on the march. Japan partnered with Nazi Germany and Italy in 1940, and the three countries formed the basis of an alliance called the Axis. They vowed to help one another in their battle for world domination.

When the Japanese military bombed Pearl Harbor in Hawaii in 1941, the United States joined Great Britain, France, the Soviet Union, and others in battling the Axis nations. (The Soviet Union, officially the Union of Soviet Socialist Republics, was a socialist state in Eurasia made up of Ukraine, Russia, Byelorussia, and Transcaucasia, with its government center in Moscow. After 1991, the USSR was dissolved and broke up into separate countries again.)

The US, Great Britain, France, and the Soviet Union were the chief countries to fight the Axis, and they were called the Allied nations. By now, nearly the entire world was at war. The conflict lasted from 1939 until 1945, when the Allies could at last claim victory. During that time, horrific numbers of people were killed, including six million Jews slaughtered by the Nazis in what became known as the Holocaust.

World War II produced many Allied heroes who proved their enormous courage and selflessness in land, air, and sea combat. But many other battles were played out—and won—in secret, by mysterious means, fought by warriors most of us have never even heard of. These were the soldiers of the underground, the Resistance fighters, and the spies who risked their lives on dangerous missions to gather information, to spread disinformation, to sabotage, confound, or destroy the enemy, all in an effort to help win the war.

This army of secret warriors was made up of all sorts of unsung heroes, from everyday citizens spying on their neighbors in broad daylight to trained soldiers and spies sneaking into enemy territory.

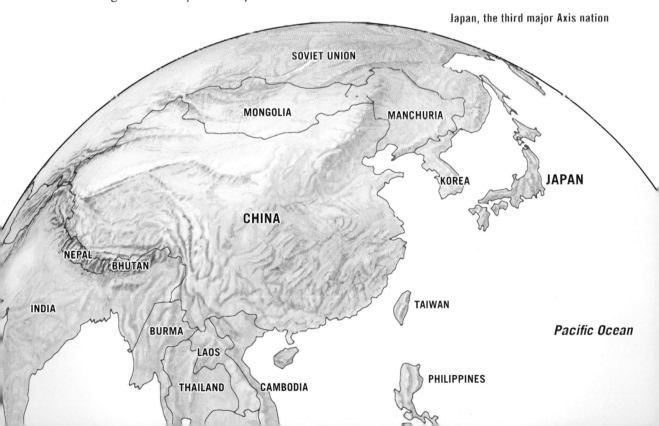

Japan, the third major Axis nation

EMPEROR HIROHITO of Japan on his favorite horse, Shirayuki, in 1935

This book profiles several such underground fighters, and the true identities of some of these spies may surprise you. Most of them had a network aiding their cause: a handler, or contact person, back home whose job was to support them as much as possible; a courier, who would deliver messages, letters, and packages; and subagents, who reported to them. There also were cryptologists who worked hard to break codes and decipher secret messages, and wireless operators who helped to send encrypted messages. And of course, all the while, there were the soldiers on the front lines.

But in the end, each spy was alone. They had to hide their work from their families and friends, in addition to the enemy. They operated in a secret world that they created themselves. They might use a false identity that had to be backed up with an entirely fabricated story. Or they might wear a disguise that had to be realistic enough to fool the people who wanted them dead. Most of all, they had to be very brave—even when facing torture and possible death.

Here are the stories of several of these surprising spies and heroes. Each was courageous in his or her own way, and they all deserve to be remembered for their efforts—and in some cases, their ultimate sacrifice.

ONE

Juan Pujol Garcia
STORYTELLER SPY

"SATANIC SPLENDOR"

Like a gang of murderous bullies, the Nazi army began its march across Europe in 1940. Juan Pujol Garcia wouldn't stand for it. He didn't hate the German people, but he couldn't tolerate what he called Hitler's "satanic splendor." How could he agree with anyone who believed in hurting people just because they were Jewish?

Juan was a Spaniard from Barcelona. He was a pacifist, which means he didn't believe in fighting with weapons or using violence to solve problems. He was "against all tyranny and oppression," and he vowed to fight the Nazis with "the only weapons at my disposal." Instead of guns, Juan had another kind of powerful weapon: he was a terrific storyteller—and he knew it.

In early 1941, Spain had not officially taken a side in the war, and Germany left the country alone. But many other European nations that had declared neutrality were still invaded by Germany—and they fell to the Nazis, alongside France and the Netherlands, which had formally declared war on Hitler. That left Britain: the only European country at war with Germany still standing. So Juan went to the British embassy in Madrid to offer his help as a spy. He asked the receptionist there if he could have a confidential meeting with one of the high-level diplomats. He refused to say what it was about. His request was passed from receptionist to secretary to clerk. Then he was told that he should write a detailed letter about his intentions and it would be given to the right person. Juan knew that it could be dangerous to put his ideas in writing. He had to come up with another plan.

That's when he had his brainstorm. His wife agreed that it was a great idea. He would offer to spy for the Germans, instead. Once they trusted him, he would give all of their secrets to the British. That would be the best way for him to fight against Hitler. But first he had to get his story straight, and to do that, he had to study Nazi **propaganda**.

Juan memorized many of the hateful things Hitler said. Then he phoned the German embassy and asked to speak to the military attaché. He told the attaché that he believed in everything the Nazis stood for and he wanted to help them. He threw in some Nazi phrases he had memorized, to show how serious he was. He was told to call back the next day. When he did, the receptionist told him to go to a certain cafe at 4:30 on the following afternoon, to meet a contact. The receptionist described the contact and asked Juan what he looked like and what he would be wearing, so that the contact would be able to recognize him.

When Juan met his contact, he explained how much he believed in the Nazi cause and repeated some more of the Nazi propaganda he had memorized. As Juan later explained, "I

began to make use of my gift of gab and ranted away as befitted a staunch Nazi." It worked, because his contact suggested that they meet again in two days to continue their conversation.

At their next meeting, his contact told him that he hoped Juan could get them "material that would be of use to the Abwehr." The Abwehr was Nazi Germany's intelligence service, and Juan assured the contact that "if they could get me a job as a foreign correspondent for a Spanish newspaper or magazine, I had what was nec-

Jewish-run businesses were targeted by the Nazis. In this photo, Nazi storm troopers are putting up a sign on the front of a Jewish business that reads "Not one penny to the Jews."

essary to travel to Britain, namely a passport. Once there, I'd be able to obtain information for them."

Juan even showed a pass he had **forged**, and claimed that it gave him permission to travel to England. Of course, he was making it all up. He had no way of getting to England. But he would figure something out.

Juan and the contact shook hands on the deal.

INVISIBLE INK, SECRET MESSAGES, AND LOTS OF LIES

A FORGED document is one that is fake, and has been made to look like the real thing. At the time Juan began spying, documents were required for nearly everything, such as permission to travel. These documents were usually made with special paper, validated with government-issued rubber stamps, and signed by an official. Anything from a passport to a letter to an identity card might be forged. It took special skills to forge a document that could pass for the real thing.

The Germans assigned Juan a **handler**, who would be his new contact. They would send Juan to Lisbon, Portugal. From there, he could make his way to England. His mission was to infiltrate regular daily life there and learn everything he could. What were the English like? What were they saying about Germany? What were their strengths and weaknesses? What were they doing to prepare for war? What kind of war equipment and machinery were they making? His Abwehr handler told him to mail his reports to a post office box in Lisbon, where they would be picked up.

Now it was time for the spying basics. The Nazis gave Juan the equivalent of $3,000 (USD) in cash, some codes, and a bottle of **invisible ink** for writing his top-secret reports. Juan rolled up the money and stuffed half of it into an empty

Every spy has a HANDLER. The handler is the person to whom a spy reports. The handler is responsible for making sure a spy has everything he or she needs, and takes special care to make sure their agent is safe.

toothpaste tube and the other half into an empty shaving-cream tube. That way, he could smuggle it from Spain into Portugal.

When he got to Portugal, he bought a British tourist guide, a train schedule, and a map of

Great Britain. He studied them. "Then, in October 1941," Juan remembered, "I sent my first message to the Germans . . . [pretending that] I was already in England. It was quite a long message."

It was a long message in part because it contained two different letters. First, Juan wrote a seemingly normal, newsy letter in regular ink. Between the lines of that letter, he then used invisible ink to write his secret message to the Nazis. In this message, Juan told the Nazis a big lie. He wrote that he had met a pilot who agreed to be a **courier** for him. The pilot offered to bring Juan's reports from England to Lisbon. There, he would deliver the letters to the post office box, where the Nazis could pick them up. It would be much quicker than mailing them from England. Of course there was no courier, no pilot. It was all made up. Juan himself was dropping the letters off in the post office box. But this way the Nazis wouldn't wonder why his reports didn't have British stamps on them.

The best way to keep a secret message secret is to make sure nobody else can read it. During World War II, many secret messages were written in INVISIBLE INK. The ink seemed to disappear when it dried, and could not be read unless it was treated with a special solution. Some kinds of invisible ink become visible when heated.

If the Nazis found out that Juan was still in Lisbon and that he was lying, that would be the end of him. It was a tremendous risk. But Juan was a natural storyteller, and the Nazis were sucked right in. They gave him the code name Agent Arabel and asked him for more information. When that happened, Juan recalled, "I had become a real German spy."

A COURIER is a messenger. Couriers deliver messages, letters, and packages to and from agents.

FAKE REPORTS TO THE NAZIS

Now that he had tricked the Nazis, Juan went to the British embassy in Lisbon. Juan was sure that once the officials there heard his story, they would bring him to England. Then his wife and son could join him there, and he could continue to write his fake reports for the Abwehr. He would give the British any information he learned about the Nazis.

But the British still refused to see him.

Juan couldn't understand why.

In fact, the British were under strict orders from their government not to do anything to involve Spain in the war. Because Spain had not entered the war, the UK had to respect Spain's position or risk creating an international incident. Since Juan was Spanish, the British couldn't work with him. But of course Juan didn't know this. All he knew was that he was still stuck in Lisbon and nobody would help him. He had to write his reports to the Nazis or else his life would be in danger. The problem was, he had never been to England. He had no idea what it was really like there, and he had no way of getting there to find out.

That's when Juan's imagination and his way with words really blossomed. He didn't want to give the Nazis any information that might harm the British, but he had to tell them something, or else they might get suspicious. He decided that he could make up his reports! He bought British newspapers and reference books and studied them for ideas. Then he wrote three more letters to his Nazi handler.

In his first letter, he wrote that he had recruited three **subagents** who would supply him with vital information.

In his second letter, he told the Nazis that he'd been offered a job with the British Broadcasting Company. The BBC was in charge of all radio and television broadcasts in England.

And in his third letter, he made up a story about five troop ships that had left England bound for Malta.

He also described what England was like. He made up what he thought British people would think and say. He wrote about things that would have sounded silly to someone in England, and he made some whopping mistakes about British currency, customs, and weather. He had no idea he was making such huge blunders, since he wasn't actually there. Fortunately for him, neither were the Nazis.

A SUBAGENT is recruited by an agent and reports only to that agent. An agent might have several subagents to help gather information and carry out tasks. Juan Pujol Garcia (Agent Arabel) had the most subagents ever recorded: twenty-seven of them. However, his subagents were not real; he made them all up.

Juan's stories were going over so well with the Germans that his handler kept asking him for further details. Pretty soon it was getting harder and harder for Juan to come up with new reports. He started to panic. What if they found out that he was still in Lisbon? What if they found out that he was making everything up? How long could he keep pretending?

Finally he decided to go to the American embassy in Lisbon, where he was able to meet with officials. He told them the whole story and asked for their help. The Americans contacted their allies at the British embassy, who suddenly realized that the information the Americans were giving them about Juan was the key to solving a problem that British Intelligence had been puzzling over for some time.

The British secret service had been listening in on the messages going in and out of Germany. Many of those messages were about someone called Agent Arabel, a Nazi spy working **undercover** in England. The British were hoping to find this Agent Arabel and turn him into a **double agent**, a spy secretly working for the British but pretending to work for the Germans. But the British hadn't been able to find him—until now. They realized that this Spaniard was the mysterious Agent Arabel. And he was right there in Lisbon.

Although he was Spanish, Juan was far too important for the British not to support his efforts. The British brought Juan and his family to England. **MI5**, the British secret service in charge of security in Britain, trained him to be more effective as a double agent, to spy on the Nazis for them. They gave him the code name Agent Garbo, after Greta

When a spy is working UNDERCOVER, it means the spy is using some sort of disguise or false identity. The agent is pretending to be someone else, so that nobody knows they're really working as a spy. Many spies used a cover identity as a writer or journalist. That way, they had a good excuse to snoop around and talk to lots of people to get information.

A DOUBLE AGENT is a spy who is working for one side but pretends to work for the other side. For instance, say a German spy is caught by the British and they convince him to spy for England instead. The spy will pretend to continue to work for the Germans, but will actually report back to England. He has become a double agent. In Juan Pujol Garcia's case, he became a double agent for England on purpose.

Garbo. She was considered to be the greatest actress in the world. It would take tremendous acting skills for Agent Garbo to continue to pull this off without getting caught.

AN ARMY OF MAKE-BELIEVE SPIES

Juan had already pretended to recruit three subagents while he was back in Lisbon. But the Nazis expected him to recruit many more, because by expanding his contacts, Juan could gather a wider range of information. So once again, Juan let loose his creative skills.

JUAN PUJOL GARCIA (Agent Garbo)

He invented a girlfriend who worked as a secretary in the British War Office. She leaked top-secret information to him. He claimed that she especially liked him because he was so attentive to her.

He dreamed up subagents in Scotland who reported back to him whenever they saw British naval exercises or troops training.

Other sources he invented included a talkative American sergeant, an anti-British waiter from Gibraltar who hated the English weather, an Indian poet, a Venezuelan student, and several members of a Welsh cult. Talk about imaginary friends!

Juan wrote up his fake subagents' findings in his reports. When necessary, his subagents led him to new "recruits," and soon he had a vast army of subagents. They would "do" whatever he needed them to do. If the Germans asked for information about airplanes, all he had to do was "recruit" a pilot or mechanic. If he needed someone who knew about manufacturing, he could "recruit" someone from a factory.

Juan was clever and creative. He invented entire lives for every one of his subagents. He

Western Europe, where JUAN PUJOL GARCIA was based—and told his stories

wrote to the Germans about how he had found each one, where he met with them, what they reported to him, and why they were willing to spy for the Nazis. Juan even wrote up their actual reports to pass along to the Nazis. Naturally, each report was written in the voice and handwriting style of a different made-up subagent, thanks to the British army. Juan later explained that "the 'appointed scribes' [were] active British soldiers who were asked [by MI5] to write the letters of any imaginary subagents; if a subagent's handwriting looked the same as the spy's, Berlin would grow suspicious. When a scribe died—taking with him his inimitable longhand—

the fake subagent often had to be killed off, unless a man with the exact same cursive style could be found quickly."

Sometimes Juan complained about them. From time to time he told the Nazis that he disagreed with things his subagents reported to him. Writing about one subagent, Juan called him "a simpleton. I am very disgusted with him, though I have not let him know this."

NEW STORIES EVERY DAY

Juan and his wife and son lived in a little house in the suburbs of London, and he commuted by train into London every day to work. His neighbors had no idea he was a spy. They thought he was just a quiet Spanish gentleman who worked at the BBC. Nobody knew that he didn't work there at all. Instead, he spent all day every day making up stories with his MI5 handler. Between the two of them, they ultimately came up with a network of twenty-seven different subagents for Juan—and all of them were invented to make the Nazis believe whatever MI5 wanted them to believe.

It was a lot to keep straight. All the stories had to sound real. Each one had to make the other stories sound just convincing enough to be believable, but not too perfect   or else the Nazis might become suspicious.

Juan wrote up long reports for the Nazis, in a complicated, flowery style. He used as many words as possible, to make them look impressive. But, as samples of his letters show, all those words didn't really say very much. There was a lot of passion in them, but not a whole lot of facts. He also included comments that echoed Nazi sentiment, in order to keep up the pretense that he agreed with them. For instance, in one of his reports he wrote, "I am certain you will be able to terrify this very pusillanimous people who will never admit that they are beaten."

Although Juan never provided anything truly useful to the Nazis, he still managed to snow them. They thought his reports were a gold mine of information. Their Agent Arabel was one of their most highly valued spies. Even Hitler was impressed with him. Some of Juan's reports were repeated word for word at the highest level of Nazi power. Boy, were the people at MI5 happy! And Juan was very pleased that his words had so much influence.

EXCERPTS FROM JUAN PUJOL GARCIA'S REPORTS

"I have observed during my walks in the centre of London that there are many American uniforms to be seen. I have also made a slight study of the activity of the Home Guard here, and I have found out that they do their training on Wednesdays and Fridays in the afternoons, and also on Sundays."

"In a French restaurant where I was dining yesterday, invited on account of my recent publication by an English official of the Ministry of Information who has lived a long time in France, I was introduced on leaving to a French friend of his dressed in the uniform of the French Air Force and wearing on his shoulder a parachute embroidered in white."

"Are you not aware of the War Office and General Staff organization? It is now almost a year that these Departments, in order to avoid espionage have been using numbers of the war units, nevertheless, these had no numbers visible, but names. As you gave me numbers in your references when I left Madrid, I, of course, supposed that you were aware of their meanings and therefore, I myself as well as my Agents have tried to obtain the numbers of the units, which is much more difficult work. I can prove what I say, as there were orders issued to this effect and one of which I obtained during my journey. Let me know how I can send this to you."

"In my next letter I shall enclose a letter addressed to the Swiss which the neutral person will hand over to him and he will speak Spanish, but his French is quite understandable, he also speaks English and I believe, although I do not know for certain, he also knows some German. However, I would advise the person who is going to get in touch with him to speak in French. Please note the following carefully. Although I am not aware of his feelings in this war I believe nevertheless, from what his friend my Agent has told me, that he is not very sympathetic towards the Axis. I make this remark so that he should be as reserved as possible and so avoid complications and getting mixed up in the matter. The Swiss has already been warned that the books will be collected from him by a man who will then take them to my wife who is going to study them with the object of writing and publishing a book shortly."

"I am not sending the letter today, but I am warning you so that you do not try and develop the letter for secret writing, as there will be none at the back, naturally."

KILLING OFF A SUBAGENT AND BREAKING GERMAN CODES

From time to time, the Germans wanted to meet one of Juan's subagents. Sometimes they were so impressed with a subagent's work that they wanted to thank the agent for such great information. Other times, they were suspicious and wanted to check an agent out. But there *were* no subagents! What could Juan do when the Nazis wanted a meeting?

First, he would stall them. He might tell them a subagent was too busy to meet. Then he would get rid of the subagent completely. Sometimes subagents moved far away. And sometimes they died, which is exactly what happened to William Gerbers.

In 1942, before the invasion of North Africa by British and American forces, there was a buildup of troops in Liverpool, England. Juan's subagent in the area, William Gerbers, a Swiss man who lived in Liverpool, hadn't noticed a thing.

But of course he hadn't; Gerbers didn't really live in Liverpool. He lived in Juan's imagination. And Juan had never even been to Liverpool.

One day, the Nazis wanted a word with this subagent who failed to mention a British troop buildup.

No problem! Juan gave Gerbers a fatal illness and killed him off before the Germans could investigate. "I said farewell to the Swiss," he wrote in a coded message to the Germans. An **obituary** appeared in the *Liverpool Echo*, placed there by MI5. Juan's German handler even sent him a condolence letter. He said they would send some money to the widow, as thanks for her husband's work for the Nazis.

Eventually, Juan "recruited" Mr. Gerbers's widow. He said Mrs. Gerbers was an experienced radio operator. She could send his long reports to the Nazis much more quickly than if he mailed them, and she could help him translate them into code. Since there was no Mrs. Gerbers, the reports were actually encoded and transmitted by an MI5 radio operator who worked with Juan.

JUAN PUJOL GARCIA (Agent Garbo) in disguise

One of Juan's most amazing feats was to help MI5 decode German messages. Every time the Germans received his long reports, they translated them into another top-secret code before sending them on, and these codes were changed every day. MI5 was listening in on the German messages. Since MI5 knew what Juan's original messages said, they could work backward to figure out what German code was being used that day. Then they were able to decode all the other messages between the Germans.

An OBITUARY is an announcement in a newspaper about somebody's death. During World War II, obituaries and other newspaper columns were favorite places for spies and their handlers to send each other messages. They would use a prearranged code. For instance, an obituary might read "Daisy Baker, beloved wife of Fritz, died peacefully in her sleep. Funeral service will be held at Shady Elm Funeral Home, September 10, at noon." Daisy Baker might be a code name for an agent. This could be a sneaky way of arranging a secret meeting with the agent at 10 Elm Street at noon.

Secret messages might also be placed in other parts of the newspaper. For instance, a spy might place a notice in the classified ads saying "Bicycle for Sale at 23 Elm Street. $10." It wouldn't have anything to do with a bicycle; instead, it might be a message to meet at 23 Elm Street at 10:00.

JUAN'S MASTERPIECE

In May 1944, all the world was waiting for the Allies to launch a massive attack against the Nazis. Allied troops, departing from Britain, would invade Nazi-occupied France and fight the Nazis on French soil. But nobody knew where they were going to land.

Juan, of course, did.

On June 6, 1944, the date known as D-Day, Allied troops began their invasion of Normandy, a region on the northern coast of France. It was the biggest amphibious (coming from water onto land) invasion in history, and it turned the tide of the war against the Nazis. Juan's biggest coup was to help convince the Nazis that the invasion would actually take place elsewhere: at the Pas de Calais, northeast of Normandy. This deception had the code name Operation Fortitude. If it worked, Hitler would send his troops to the wrong place. That would give the Allies a fighting chance. If it didn't work, there would be too many Nazi troops for the

Allies to battle. There would be little chance of success, and many, many more people would be killed.

"The constant bombing that the area of the Pas de Calais is suffering and the strategic situation of these forces makes me suspect an attack on that French region, which is also the shortest route to their prized final objective, that is, Berlin." So read a wordy message Juan sent to the Nazis on June 9, 1944. According to the German war minister, this message convinced the Nazis to reroute most of their troops away from Normandy, despite the massive Allied offensive that had already been taking place there for three days. Operation Fortitude was a success, and even after the Normandy invasion, the Nazis continued to gather their troops at the Pas de Calais, expecting a second, even greater attack, which never came.

General Dwight D. Eisenhower, supreme commander of the US and Allied troops and later the 34th US president, observed that "lack of infantry was the most important cause of the enemy's defeat in Normandy." German Field Marshal Erwin Rommel, a favorite of Hitler's who was also known as the Desert Fox, led the German army during World War II and said that it had been "a decisive mistake to leave the German troops in the Pas de Calais."

Juan helped make possible the enormous success of the invasion, which led to the defeat of the Nazis.

Even after the Normandy invasion, the Nazis still believed that Juan had been helping them. They awarded him the Iron Cross, a distinguished medal, for his service. They never suspected that he was a double agent, working to bring them down. Juan also received a Member of the Order of the British Empire award from England, but it had to be given to him in secret, to protect his identity as a double agent.

JUAN'S DISAPPEARING ACT

In 1945, soon after the war ended, Juan and his family moved to Venezuela, where he quietly worked as a language teacher. Three years later, he and his wife separated and she moved back to Spain with their children. Juan remained in Venezuela, where, in 1959, he tricked the whole world by faking his own death. He worried that the Germans might finally realize that he had betrayed them, and he didn't want to be in danger. So he asked his former MI5 handler to spread a rumor that he had died of malaria after being bitten by a mosquito in Angola.

Twenty-five years later, in 1984, Juan was tracked down by a persistent British writer, who persuaded him to return to England. There, the British government publicly honored him for his bravery. Prince Philip presented him with the Member of the Order of the British Empire award at a special ceremony at Buckingham Palace. Finally the whole world learned about Juan Pujol Garcia, one of the most important spies of World War II, and the magnificent role he had played in helping to defeat Hitler.

Juan was like an illusionist with the way he used words and stories to trick the Nazis. But another spy used actual conjuring tricks in the fight against Hitler. His name was Jasper Maskelyne, and he was a real magician.

TWO

Jasper Maskelyne
MAGICIAN SPY

MAGIC ACT

The year was 1937. A mustachioed magician in a fancy tuxedo stood on a London stage, smiling at a movie camera. His next trick was captured on film.

"I went to my doctor the other day," the magician recounted, "and I said, 'Doctor, I don't feel very well.' He said, 'What's the matter with you?' I said, 'I can't eat properly. I wonder, could you give me a good tonic to put an edge on my appetite?' He said, 'Yes, if I were you, I'd eat a lot of razor blades every day. That ought to put an edge on your appetite.' Here," the magician said to his audience, "I'll just show you."

The magician held up a razor blade.

"Real blades. I shaved with this one this morning."

As he chatted on, he demonstrated how sharp the blade was by slashing a piece of paper to ribbons.

"If you'll pardon me, I'll just take my medicine," he said, and he placed the blade flat on the top of his tongue. He chewed and swallowed, then ate another blade and another and another.

"Don't make me laugh; I shall cut my tonsils out!"

After he'd eaten a dozen blades, he took a sip of water. Then he took a pair of scissors, snipped off a long piece from a ball of string, placed it in his mouth, and chewed it up. After another sip of water, he slowly pulled the string out of his mouth, and presto! All twelve blades were threaded on the string in a row. It was all in a day's work for Jasper Maskelyne.

FROM LONDON STAGE TO WORLD STAGE

Magicians are experts at camouflage and diversion. That's how they trick us into seeing only what they want us to see. Jasper Maskelyne was a master illusionist and an expert at sleight of hand. That's what it's called when a magician uses fast and tricky hand movements to make things like cards or coins seem to appear and disappear. Jasper's son, Alistair, remembered his father's incredible talent well. "He had this ability to conceal things when people were looking straight at them. Now, that is the art of camouflage."

Jasper Maskelyne was also a show-off. He liked to dress up in a top hat and fancy suit, and he loved performing. He had a high opinion of himself—and rightly so: he was the most famous magician in London, talented and successful, just like his father and grandfather before him. His razor-blade-swallowing trick was an audience favorite. But by the late 1930s, after a successful sixty-year run, the Maskelyne family magic shows were no longer attracting a huge audience, thanks largely to Hitler's rise and the threat of war.

In October 1940, Jasper signed up for the British army. He wanted to fight Hitler. But at age thirty-seven, he was a little old for combat. Instead, the army placed him in the Royal Engineers, and he began training.

JASPER MASKELYNE in his Royal Engineers uniform. This photo is inscribed to his wife and daughter.

THE MAGIC GANG

Even though he wasn't going to the front lines, Jasper was sure that he could figure out a way to use his talents of deception to help the British defeat the Nazis and save lives. "If I could stand in the focus of powerful footlights and deceive attentive and undisturbed onlookers, separated from me only by the width of the orchestra pit, then I could most certainly devise means of deceiving German observers a mile away or more," he claimed.

Eventually the army assigned him to the camouflage unit, where Jasper hoped to put his tactics as a magician to work. The problem was, Jasper's fellow soldiers weren't ready for Jasper's outrageous ideas. Sure, they knew about using paint to make a tank look like part of the surrounding scenery. But using magic tricks to fight a war or to make an army vanish? Nonsense.

Nothing fazed Jasper, least of all his doubting comrades. When he found out that the inspector general of the British army was coming to the base to observe a military exercise, he realized this could be his chance! As the inspector general walked across the training field, looking for Jasper's machine-gun bunker, Jasper lay in wait. The inspector general knew it was there somewhere, but he simply couldn't see it. Then—presto!—the bunker appeared out of nowhere, with a machine gun (actually a broomstick) aimed right at him. Bang!

It was an impressive trick. Using his knowledge of stage magic, Jasper had made a machine-gun bunker seem to vanish and then reappear. The inspector general realized that this magician just might be useful after all. He sent Jasper to the British army's camouflage unit in the Western Desert in North Africa, in December 1940.

The North African campaign of World War II had started earlier that year when Italy declared war in the region. For the next three years, battles would rage in the Libyan and Egyptian deserts and in Morocco, Algeria, and Tunisia. Great Britain and France helped fight the Nazis and Italians in North Africa, and the US joined the Allies there in 1942. When Jasper was sent to the region, he was told to entertain the troops with his magic act. But he was also ordered to put together a team and await instructions.

Jasper was enthusiastic. As much as he loved performing magic, this was war. He still had big ideas about using deception to fight the enemy, and now he would have a team to help him. He called his team the Magic Gang, and it was made up of misfits and oddballs, including a chemist, a carpenter, a cartoonist, an electrical engineer, a stage designer, a criminal, and an art restorer.

CAMEL DUNG AND EXPLODING RATS

The Magic Gang was bored and restless as they waited for their orders. Then they finally got their first assignment: they were to create special camouflage paint for 238 British tanks. It wasn't very exciting, but at least it was something to do—and it did present a unique challenge. The tanks had been painted green, because they were originally supposed to be used in a place that had a lot of trees and fields. But the desert isn't green. And Jasper's Magic Gang didn't have any paint.

Fortunately, they had a chemist and a couple of artists in their ranks. They would make their own paint. They poked around in an old military dump and found oil drums filled with Worcestershire sauce, and bags of cement and spoiled flour. When mixed together, this made a perfect base for their paint. Unfortunately, the color turned out to be a muddy red, which is as useless in the desert as green. They needed pigment to make it the right color.

The Magic Gang was in North Africa, based in the desert, with camels all around. They couldn't just drive to an art supply store for pigment. It was 1941, and the internet hadn't been invented yet, so they couldn't order pigment online. They would have to figure out a solution themselves. They thought and thought about what they might try. Eventually they realized that the perfect ingredient was right there beneath their feet: camel droppings.

They did some experiments. They found that when they mixed camel dung into the base paint, it created the perfect color—although it was very smelly. (After drying out for a few days, the smell wasn't quite as bad.) They would have to collect an enormous amount of droppings, so they formed a Dung Patrol. As Jasper said, "We stand behind every camel."

After the success of their paint job, the Magic Gang came up with an assortment of other weapons and devices. They disguised land mines by hiding them in piles of camel dung. They also packed explosives into dead rats and left them out where an unsuspecting Nazi might drive over them.

SOME GREAT INVENTIONS

In addition to being a famous magician, Jasper was also an inventor—his most successful **invention** was the coin-operated lock for a toilet-stall door. So the British army offered him five British pounds for any new invention he could come up with.

He invented a toothbrush that had a hidden map, compass, and hacksaw inside; a cigarette holder that was actually a miniature telescope; a fountain pen that fired tear gas; shoelace tips that doubled as compass needles, and maps that could be hidden inside the tongue of a boot; codes for secret messages written on a piece of string—they looked like dots, but when the string was wound several times around a soldier's belt, the message became clear; a map made from rice paper and sprayed with a coating of vegetable oil, which made

Jasper's INVENTIONS weren't the only gadgets used by spies and soldiers. Throughout history, spies have relied on various gizmos to help them do their jobs and stay safe. These include such weapons as a glove pistol, which is exactly what it sounds like: a small pistol partially concealed in a glove; a lipstick pistol; and lethal blades or poisoned spikes concealed at the tip of an umbrella. Messages and items such as weapons, maps, or supplies could be hidden inside fake rocks or secreted in hidden compartments. A miniature camera could be hidden in a handbag or briefcase, in a pen or a cigarette lighter, or even in the button or belt buckle of a coat. Film with secret information could be made smaller and and smaller until it would fit on a tiny dot, which could then be hidden under a postage stamp or inside a hollow coin or ring. Someone even invented an artificial eye that could be worn something like a contact lens, to hide and transport a microdot of secret information.

When he was in Egypt in September 1941, JASPER MASKELYNE wrote in a letter to his wife and daughter, "I've invented a fireproof cream which has cut out the asbestos suit. Any chump can make it! With a boiler suit dipped in it, and a wet towel round your head, you can walk right into a burning aeroplane and rescue the crew." This photo shows the fireproof cream being applied to a man sitting in a washtub. He's wearing goggles to protect his eyes.

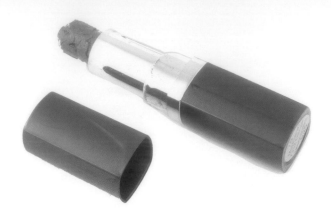

Many objects, such as this lipstick, were specially made with a hidden compartment for spies to conceal small items.

it waterproof and also made it easier to eat, in case its owner was captured by the enemy; and, perhaps most important, a fire-resistant paste—especially useful for pilots to smear on, in case of a fiery crash.

He also agreed to give talks on escape and evasion, demonstrating useful techniques. As a magician who knew how to free himself from tightly knotted ropes and escape from a locked box, he had a lot of tricks up his sleeve. Most magicians won't tell their secrets, but Jasper was eager to share some of his in the war against Hitler.

A COMMAND PERFORMANCE FOR A KING, AND A SECRET MISSION

In his memoir, Jasper described being sent on a spy mission for **MI9**, a special section of British Military Intelligence, in November 1941, while he was stationed in North Africa. Although some historians think he may have exaggerated his role, this is what he claimed happened:

MI9 was a specialized department of the British Directorate of Military Intelligence, part of the War Office, in operation from 1939 to 1945. MI9 was in charge of helping British prisoners of war escape, and helped to bring back to Britain any British soldiers or airmen who had been shot down or stranded in enemy-occupied territory. MI9 also tried to stay in contact with British prisoners of war, and sent them packages that had hidden in them all sorts of escape aids, including lock-picking equipment and maps as well as forged German ID cards and ration coupons, weapons, etc.

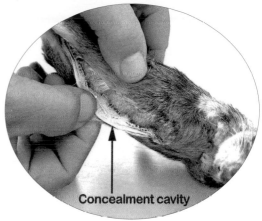

Dead rats were used as dead drops—a way of hiding a message or small item so that nobody else would find it except the spy for whom it was intended. It was very effective: Who would want to examine a dead rat?

Concealment cavity

You can see the concealment cavity in this dead rat.

Jasper had been told that there was a hidden radio transmitter somewhere in Cairo that was sending messages to the enemy. It had to be found. MI9 suspected that it was in King Farouk's palace. But intelligence officers from MI9 couldn't just go into the king of Egypt's home and search for it; if they didn't find it, it would create a terrible political scandal.

King Farouk loved magic and spectacle, so the plan was for Jasper to do a special magic show at the palace, especially for the king. The magic show would be a diversion, to keep the king and his guards busy. That would give Jasper an opportunity to search for the radio.

He came up with a great show. He would do some fancy magic tricks, and then he would perform one of his most exciting escape tricks. That would keep the audience riveted.

His assistants made a big deal of tying him up in chains and ropes. Then he was placed in a cabinet, which was locked. The king himself turned the key to lock it, and held on to the key. Then the audience waited, while music played. Inside the cabinet, Jasper quickly slipped out of his bonds and escaped through a hidden panel. He began to search the palace while all eyes were on the locked cabinet. The clock ticked, and he tiptoed from room to room, looking for the radio.

Finally, he found it in a storage room. He rushed back to the cabinet and slipped back in through the panel, just as the king was getting ready to unlock the cabinet. When the door opened, out popped Jasper, magically freed from his bonds. Ta-da!

According to Jasper, the king loved the show. And Jasper reported back to MI9, letting them know where the radio was located. The next morning, troops came to King Farouk's palace to confiscate the transmitter.

PRESTO! SAVE THE SUEZ CANAL

By 1941, Germany and Italy had taken over almost all of North Africa, but Hitler couldn't get his hands on Egypt and the Suez Canal. The Suez Canal was a one-hundred-mile waterway that linked the Mediterranean to the Red Sea. If Hitler could destroy the canal, then the Nazis would be able to control shipping from the oil fields in the Middle East. This would cripple the British army, as Middle Eastern oil was their major source of fuel.

Jasper claimed that he had a major role in protecting the Suez Canal. It was impossible to defend the Suez Canal, since it was simply too long. But Jasper knew that he could hide it—or make it seem to disappear. If a magician wants something to vanish, he uses a special magic trick: lights are shone directly at the audience, which makes everything behind the lights impossible to see. Try it out with friends and you'll see—or not!

The German LUFTWAFFE (German for "air weapon") was created in 1935, and by 1940 it had become Europe's biggest and most powerful air force.

Jasper took credit for inventing and building a series of dazzle-lights that would spin around to reflect light up into the sky in whirling circles. The effect—somewhat like a strobe light—would blind Hitler's air force, the **Luftwaffe**, and if they couldn't see their target, they wouldn't be able to bomb it.

The Germans never did close down the Suez Canal. While there is no official acknowledgment of any role Jasper may have had, he claimed that his whirling sprays of light saved it.

Jasper also claimed that he saved the port of Alexandria from night bombing by the Nazis. Supposedly he and his men built a dummy port at the nearby Bay of Maryut, trying to make it look exactly like the Alexandrian port. The idea was that when the lights were all turned off at Alexandria at night, the Nazis would mistake the lit dummy port for the real thing and bomb it instead. However, once again, there is no proof that this illusion ever actually happened, despite Jasper's claims.

Dummy tanks were built over trucks to fool the Nazis.

HOW TO MAKE AN ARMY VANISH

It was 1941, and Rommel, the Nazis' Desert Fox, was getting ready to wage a major attack in North Africa. That's what Allied spies were reporting. But the British stationed there weren't in a position to defend themselves. They were waiting for reinforcements. It would take at least

A crew fits a cover onto a tank to disguise it as a truck.

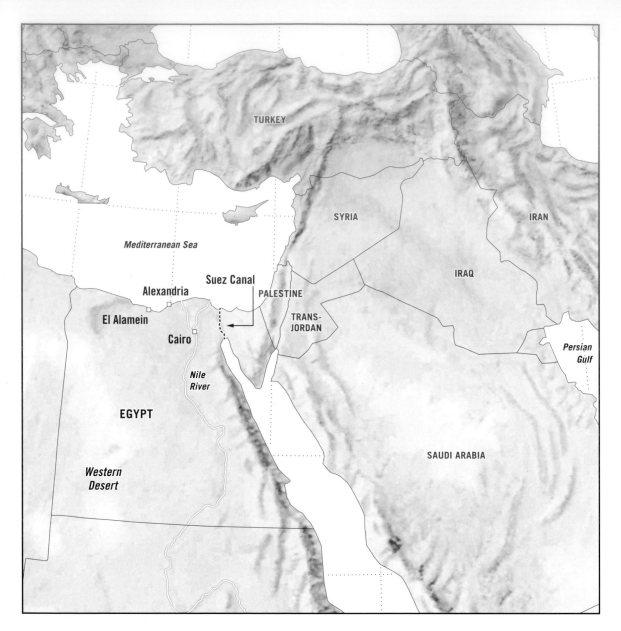

The Middle East and the region of North Africa where JASPER MASKELYNE helped trick the Nazis

another two months before they had enough troops and weapons to prevent Rommel's advance. Jasper's gang would really have to work their magic this time, or else the Nazis would take over all of North Africa.

The first thing the British needed was more soldiers. So the Magic Gang made them. They built dummy soldiers, using canvas and cardboard and tubes and whatever else they had. They painted the dummies and clothed them in old pieces of uniforms and fabric that was painted to look like uniforms. The dummy soldiers were posed in different positions—resting, sitting, standing—and placed among the real soldiers, to make it look like there was a much bigger army. They also made fake tents out of cardboard and canvas, and set up extra campfires, to make it look real.

The Magic Gang disguised trucks as tanks and tanks as trucks, using clever flaps and removable coverings. When a tank was disguised as a truck, the telltale track of the tank treads also had to be disguised. Hanging a chain-link flap to drag in the sand behind a tank would erase the tread marks and make it look like tire tracks instead. The British could use them wherever needed, to fool the enemy. The Nazis would never be able to tell whether they were simply moving supply trucks, or if they were amassing tanks in preparation for an attack.

Even with a dummy army, the British would have to do a lot more to keep Rommel from attacking. Word was that Rommel would attack in the north, at El Alamein. If so, the Nazis would slaughter the small group of British forces there. General Montgomery, who was in charge of the British troops, went to Jasper to ask for his help in fooling Rommel. If Jasper could convince Rommel to bring most of his troops to attack in a different spot, the British might be able to defend themselves in the north. Jasper would have to find a way to trick Rommel.

How do you convince a crafty, battle-tested general that you have a huge army ready to attack, when really the army is in another place altogether? And how do you keep the real army hidden from view? "You must conceal one hundred fifty thousand men with a thousand guns and a thousand tanks on a plain as hard and flat as a billiard table, and the Germans must not know anything about it, although they will be watching every movement, listening for every noise, charting every track. . . . You can't do it, of course, but you've bloody well got to," said Montgomery's chief of staff.

And they bloody well did! Under Jasper's direction, they amassed a huge number of tanks to prepare for battle, then disguised them as trucks. They also hid ammunition, guns, and supplies under cardboard and canvas creations painted to look like trucks. If Rommel's army flew overhead, they'd see lots of trucks parked, and wouldn't realize what was underneath.

Meanwhile, to the south, the British pretended to amass tanks and soldiers and ammunition and supplies, but they were mostly dummies, which got moved around from time to time to make them look real. They even built a fake pipeline, from crushed tin gasoline cans, to make it look like they were piping in water for a huge army. They made very slow progress on the fake pipeline, in order to convince the Nazis that they weren't yet ready to do battle. Rommel was completely unprepared when the attack came; most of his troops were in the wrong place, at the wrong time.

Jasper's team and their magic tricks helped the British to their first big win against the Nazis in North Africa, boosting morale and helping lead to victory.

A GOOD MAGICIAN NEVER REVEALS ALL OF HIS SECRETS

After the war, Jasper returned to England for a few years, then moved with his family to Kenya. When he died in 1973, he left the world with a great mystery. His memoirs describe many of his adventures during the war, written with his flair for braggadocio. We know he did a lot of exciting things, but he also may have exaggerated some of his heroic exploits and inventions. Which were real and which were trickery? We'll never know for sure.

Jasper was a confident, boastful performer who used his magic to hide armies and fool a king. Another performer, the American dancer and singer Josephine Baker, used her tremendous fame to dazzle her admirers while hiding her undercover activities for the French Resistance.

THREE

SMUGGLED PETS AND SECRET MESSAGES

Madame was not allowed to take an animal on board the ship, according to the customs officials. But nobody, not even customs officials, told the great Josephine Baker what she could or couldn't do. La Baker, as she was known in France, was one of the most famous dancers in the world. She would do whatever she wanted. And there was no way she was going to travel without taking her beloved dog with her.

The ship's crew could at least be glad that she didn't have any of her other pets with her. Over the years, Josephine kept pet monkeys, dogs, cats, pigs, mice, rabbits, goldfish, snakes, and birds. They lived with her in her hotel rooms and her home, and she loved them all. She thought of them as her children, and they made her laugh with joy.

It wasn't unusual to spot Josephine with her pet snake, Kiki, draped around her throat. "He was adorable," she remembered, "just long enough to knot himself around my neck like a collar. He loved to lie there warm and snug, and looked just right with my favorite black velvet dress." For a while, she had a pet cheetah that performed with her in some of her shows. She put Chiquita in a diamond-studded collar and leash, and they made quite a sight walking together through the streets of Paris. Sometimes her pet chimpanzee, Ethel, joined them on their walks, too, dressed in a diamond choker and bracelets.

She always had animals with her at home, and whenever she could, she brought some of them along when she traveled—even when it was forbidden.

And so, as she prepared to travel from Algeria back to France after the liberation of Paris in 1944, when nobody was looking she stuffed her little black-and-white puppy under her coat and smuggled it on board the ship. The puppy quickly became the ship's mascot, and none of her fellow passengers seemed to mind that Josephine had once again broken the rules.

JOSEPHINE BAKER posing with her beloved pet cheetah, Chiquita

Animals weren't the only things Josephine snuck across borders during her lifetime. She also smuggled secret messages for the **French Resistance** during World War II. Although she didn't think of herself as a spy (her official title was "**honorable correspondent**"), she actually did the dangerous work of a spy. She furtively gathered and transported crucial information for the Resistance. Her role was secret and perilous, and she willingly risked her life to help defeat the Nazis. If she had been caught, even the great Josephine Baker would have gone to prison—or worse.

But unlike many spies, she didn't hide herself from the authorities. She could never have hidden her identity or traveled in disguise; she was much too famous and recognizable.

The FRENCH RESISTANCE was made up of dedicated men and women who worked undercover, outside of the regular French army, doing everything possible to defy and disrupt the Nazis. They were people of all kinds and all ages—some were just kids. They spread disinformation and passed along secret messages. They created and distributed false identity papers, and helped lead refugees and stranded pilots to safety. They received secret parachute drops of weapons and supplies from England and North Africa. They also sabotaged railway lines and bombed bridges to cripple the Nazi transport system. Sometimes they even executed collaborators whose treachery had caused others to be arrested or killed.

Instead, she used her great fame to her advantage. No one would ever suspect La Baker of hiding anything. She was famous for baring her body onstage. Why would she conceal anything? Nobody would dare to search her, she always said. Nobody would suspect that she was a spy.

And she was right.

But who was this brave diva? How did a poor African American woman who grew up under the brutal segregationist laws of the Jim Crow era end up being the most famous dancer in the world? And how did La Baker become a French spy?

GROWING UP IN POVERTY

Josephine was born Freda Josephine McDonald in 1906 in St. Louis, Missouri, where most African American residents lived in extreme poverty. Her father left when she was a baby, and though her mother soon remarried, her stepfather didn't have a job. So it was up to her mother to raise and support Josephine and her three siblings, with some help from their grandmother.

HONORABLE CORRESPONDENTS were a special brand of spy. The French Resistance was always looking for volunteers who could get visas easily and could therefore travel freely without drawing suspicion to themselves. Their role was to deliver messages and gather information for the Deuxième Bureau—French Intelligence under General Charles de Gaulle's Free French Forces.

Her mother washed other people's clothes to make a living, and Josephine helped. She also shoveled snow, worked as a housekeeper and a waitress, and did other chores to help her mother pay the bills and feed the family. This was in addition to caring for her younger siblings, which she did from the age of five.

In St. Louis and many other places in the US at that time, black and white people were segregated. Josephine's family had to flee their home when their community was attacked during race riots in 1917. Nearly all of the buildings in their neighborhood were set on fire and burned to the ground, and the fleeing residents were attacked by an angry mob. Josephine and her family were lucky to escape. She would remember this horrific event for her entire life, and it would inspire her later work for equal rights.

A GOOFBALL AND A DANCER

When Josephine was very young, she stepped on a rusty nail and contracted blood poisoning. The doctor wanted to amputate her leg to stop the infection, but Josephine screamed and cried in protest. The doctor treated the wound instead, and it eventually healed. Thank goodness! Because Josephine wanted to be a dancer.

She had seen the performers at the black vaudeville house in St. Louis, and she wanted to do what they did: play music and dance onstage. She loved dressing up in the fancy clothes from her grandmother's trunk and putting on shows with her friends. Josephine was always dancing. Sometimes in the freezing cold winters she danced just to keep warm, but dancing also made her feel happy.

So did making people laugh. Josephine could be a real goofball, and she had a talent for physical comedy. She would cross her eyes and ham it up, arms flailing and legs kicking, sometimes crouching like a frog or springing up into the air, with great agility and always with a silly smile. She was very good at getting attention in any way she could.

When Josephine was twelve, she joined a small band. She didn't get paid, but she learned to sing, play the trombone, and hone her dancing skills. Best of all, she got a chance to perform. When the band was invited to go on tour with another, larger band, Josephine went along with them.

By age sixteen, she was in the chorus line of a touring show called *Shuffle Along*. She drew attention to herself by doing the opposite of what everyone else was doing. She goofed around, shimmying and making faces, and the audience laughed and laughed. The other performers were annoyed that she was hogging the spotlight, but the audience loved her!

PARIS: OOH LÀ LÀ!

Before long, Josephine was recruited to join a show featuring other black performers in Paris, France. Interest in black culture was growing in the country, and jazz music, African American dance, and African art and culture were becoming increasingly popular. *La Revue Nègre* (*The Negro Revue*) opened in 1925, with Josephine featured on all the posters. After a few weeks dancing the Charleston in her signature style, she was cast in her groundbreaking role. Wearing nothing but a skirt of pink feathers, she was carried onto the stage by another dancer who slowly lowered her to the ground. Then she rose and danced up a storm, shaking her hips and rolling to the music. The audience went wild! They'd never seen anything like it before. Josephine was only eighteen years old, and she was a star.

Josephine loved Paris. It was the first place where she was treated with respect. Black and white people weren't segregated as they were in the US, which meant that Josephine could go to any restaurant or hotel that she liked. There were no signs saying "Whites Only" in Paris.

France became Josephine's adopted home. She learned to read and write there, and she learned to speak French. She even opened up her own nightclub in Paris. Her favorite song was "J'ai Deux Amours" (I Have Two Loves), which paid homage to her native land and her new home:

> *J'ai deux amours*
> *Mon pays et Paris.*
> *Par eux toujours*
> *Mon coeur est ravi.*

> I have two loves
> My country and Paris.
> By both of them
> My heart is ravished.

A DANCING SENSATION

The more Josephine performed, the more her fame grew. As she danced and sang in shows all over Europe, she caused a sensation everywhere she went. A newspaper review at the time described her performance as being "in constant motion. . . . Music seems to pour from her body."

By 1926, Josephine was quite possibly the richest black woman in the world, and certainly the most photographed woman of her time. With her fame and fortune, she bought beautiful clothing, fancy perfumes, and fine jewelry, and she began to acquire her collection of adored pets. She also collected admirers, and was married four times. She fell in love with many people, including the artist Pablo Picasso, the mystery writer Georges Simenon, and the French novelist Colette.

BLACK AND JEWISH

In 1928, as Nazi ideals about the purity of the Aryan race began to spread, Josephine found that some countries were becoming less welcoming. In Germany and Austria, especially, audiences shouted insults at her and even threw ammonia bombs onstage when she was performing. Their reaction may have been partly due to her revealing costumes, but it was mostly because she was a black woman onstage with white performers.

Josephine's third husband, Jean Lion, was a French Jew. When she married him in 1937, she became a French citizen and she also said that she converted to Judaism. As Hitler's influence grew, her identity as a woman who was both black and Jewish put her doubly at risk. But Josephine wasn't afraid. Instead, she vowed to take a stand against the Nazis, and she joined the International League Against Racism and Anti-Semitism. She also joined the Red Cross. Jean had taught her to fly and she had gotten her pilot's license, so she helped by flying Red Cross supplies into Belgium. She also knit socks for the soldiers. (Later, she would take her knitting along with her on missions.)

GENERAL CHARLES DE GAULLE'S FREE FRENCH FORCES were formed shortly after France negotiated an armistice with Germany in 1940 and the country was split into the northern zone, controlled by the Nazis, and the southern zone, controlled by the Vichy government under Marshal Philippe Pétain. General Charles de Gaulle was opposed to the armistice and the Vichy government. He fled to England and set up a government in exile in London. His followers were the Free French Forces, and under his leadership they fought against the Nazis.

AN HONORABLE CORRESPONDENT

In 1940, the French counterintelligence agency, the Deuxième Bureau (part of **General Charles de Gaulle's Free French Forces**) was looking for "honorable correspondents." These were volunteer undercover agents who were willing to dedicate their lives to fighting the Nazis. The bureau hoped to recruit people who could get visas easily. Visas would allow the correspondents to travel freely throughout Europe and North Africa without drawing suspicion. They could deliver messages and gather information to help the Free French Forces.

Jacques Abtey was the head of military counterintelligence in France. One of his friends knew Josephine and suggested that he meet her. She might be perfect for the job, his friend reasoned. She was accustomed to traveling for her shows and, as he told Abtey, *"C'est une femme courageuse!"* (She's a courageous woman). Abtey wasn't entirely convinced, but he decided to meet La Baker, just in case.

Their mutual friend brought Abtey to Josephine's country home, Les Milandes, and introduced Abtey under a pseudonym: Monsieur Fox. Abtey was impressed by Josephine. When he finally explained what he had in mind, she told him, "France made me what I am. I will be grateful forever. The people of Paris have given me everything. They have given me their hearts, and I have given them mine. I am ready, captain, to give them my life. You can use me as you wish." She decided that intelligence work would be "the perfect way to fight *my* war"—her battle against injustice and racism.

Not long after their conversation, Josephine reported for some basic training. She learned to speak and read both German and Italian. She was trained in karate. She was put through a battery of memory tests that challenged her to recall information for weeks at a time. She also learned to use a pistol, and was soon able to extinguish the flame from a candle with a shot from twenty yards away. She was taught to use codes and invisible ink—and to make sure she destroyed any other paper she might have used. That was the safest way to smuggle important information.

Josephine was also provided with several pills containing fatal doses of cyanide. Abtey explained that "if she ever found herself in a situation she could not handle, the capsules killed instantly. Suicide, the Resistance believed, was a noble alternative to enemy capture."

JOSEPHINE'S FIRST MISSION

In early 1940, Italy had not yet entered the war, but there were rumors that it might do so soon. The war was all anybody talked about. So Josephine's first mission was to find out more about Italy's plans. She had already attended many parties at the Italian embassy, so when she made an appearance at yet another, Josephine already knew the scene well. But this time, as she flirted and chatted with diplomats and politicians, she was really listening for military and political information, all of which she passed on to Abtey.

Not long after her first mission, the Nazis invaded Paris. Josephine vowed not to perform in France again until all the Nazis had gone. She left Paris and retired to Les Milandes, taking along three of her dogs, her maid, and a refugee Belgian couple. But she didn't stop helping the Resistance. Josephine noted, "The vast chateau with its secret nooks and crannies made an ideal hiding place. And hide we did, concealing a navy officer, an air force captain, a Pole, my Belgian friends." Not only did Josephine and her husband house refugees and Resistance members, they also hid weapons.

Soon the Germans began to get suspicious—perhaps the comings and goings at Les Milandes made them suspect something was going on there. Whatever it was that put Josephine's house on their radar was enough to make them pay a visit to Les Milandes to inspect the property. But Josephine, ever the entertainer, managed to sweet-talk them into leaving. After that, Abtey determined that it was no longer safe for her to stay at Les Milandes. It was time for Josephine to leave—on another mission.

GATHERING TOP SECRET INFORMATION

Josephine and Abtey had orders to get themselves to England, where France's leader, General de Gaulle, was living in exile and directing the Free French Forces. The pair would have to travel to Lisbon, Portugal, first, and from there they'd need to find a way to get to England. Josephine arranged to perform in some shows, and easily obtained a visa. It was a little more difficult to get a visa for Abtey, who was posing as her secretary, but Josephine made it happen. In order to avoid looking suspicious, Josephine traveled with dozens of suitcases and trunks for her costumes, and some of her animals. How many spies would draw attention to themselves like that?

Josephine and Abtey stayed for a while in Lisbon, where Josephine attended embassy parties and other events, gathering information all the while. Then their orders changed: they would not be going to England after all. They were needed elsewhere. Josephine was disappointed. She had hoped to meet General de Gaulle, who was one of her heroes. (Later, she got to meet the general when he attended one of her performances. He gave her a tiny gold Lorraine cross, the symbol of the Free French Forces, which she cherished—until she sold it to raise money for them.)

Despite her disappointment about England, Josephine gave her next assignments everything she had. "Being Josephine Baker had definite advantages," she remembered. "Seville, Madrid, Barcelona . . . wherever I went, I was swamped with invitations. I particularly liked attending diplomatic functions, since the embassies and consulates swarmed with talkative people. Back at my hotel, I carefully recorded everything I'd heard. My notes would have been highly compromising had they been discovered, but who would dare search Josephine Baker to the skin? The information remained snugly in place, secured by a safety pin." That safety pin was secured to her underwear!

Sometimes Josephine even wrote secret notes on her arms, knowing that the ink would be hidden under her sleeves. She was confident that nobody would dare to search her. "Besides, my encounters with customs officials were always extremely relaxed. When they asked *me* for papers, they generally meant autographs."

INVISIBLE INK

For her first solo mission, Josephine had to travel from Spain to North Africa so she could deliver important military secrets for the Resistance. Abtey encoded the information and used invisible ink to write it in the margins of her sheet music.

After the war, Abtey's superior said, "It can fairly be said that the destiny of our Allies and consequently of the Free French was written in part on the pages of 'Two Loves Have I.'"

SPIES AT HER BEDSIDE

In 1941, Josephine and Abtey were sent to Casablanca, in Morocco, to set up a base for their undercover operations. Josephine traveled with three monkeys, two white mice, a hamster, her Great Dane Bonzo—and twenty-eight pieces of luggage. While she was there, she fell gravely ill. For many years, she had desperately wanted to have children, but had been unable to become pregnant. A doctor performed a risky procedure to try to help her, but it caused a horrible infection. Josephine became so ill that there were even rumors she had died.

A secret message was written in invisible ink on this handkerchief. A special chemical was applied to reveal the message.

It took a long time for her to recover. Abtey spent days and nights by her side at the clinic. When she began to feel a little better, they decided to use her sickroom as a meeting place for spies to exchange information. Nobody would suspect a thing, since the great Josephine Baker would naturally have many important visitors.

BRINGING BLACKS AND WHITES TOGETHER

When Josephine had recovered, she started traveling through North Africa and the Middle East, continuing to help the Free French Forces and singing for the troops. She was given the honorary title of sublieutenant in the women's auxiliary of the French air force. She sang for American and British troops as well as the Free French Forces. But she insisted that all the audiences be integrated, with everyone sitting together. "We've got to show that blacks and whites are treated equally in the army. Otherwise, what's the point of waging war on Hitler?"

A MEDAL FROM GENERAL DE GAULLE

Paris was liberated in August 1944, and in 1945 the war ended. Josephine spent her days helping to feed the poor and raising money for war victims. In 1946 she became very ill again. In October of that year, when she was in her hospital bed, she was presented with **La Médaille de la Résistance avec le grade d'officier** (the Medal of the Resistance with Rosette) for her work helping the French Resistance. General de Gaulle's daughter presented it to her in person, along with a letter from de Gaulle. Much later, in 1961, she was also named a **Chevalier de la Légion d'Honneur** (Knight of the Legion of Honor)—the highest decoration in France—by the French government, for her hard work and dedication to France.

> LA MÉDAILLE DE LA RÉSISTANCE AVEC LE GRADE D'OFFICIER—the French Medal of the Resistance with Rosette—was an award established by General Charles de Gaulle to acknowledge remarkable acts of faith and courage that contributed to the resistance of the French people against the Axis forces after 1940.

THE RAINBOW TRIBE

Josephine married her fourth husband, Jo Bouillon, in 1947, and they settled at Les Milandes. Together they adopted twelve children of different nationalities. Josephine and Jo wanted their "Rainbow Tribe" to demonstrate to the world that all races could live together in peace.

Josephine and her family loved one another, but there was one huge source of stress: Josephine was a big spender, and she wasn't very good at budgeting. She continued to perform in order to support her family, but then she spent her earnings as soon as she had them. Much of the time she was in debt. Eventually she and Jo divorced, and she ended up losing her home. She and her children had to rely on her ex-husband and her friends to support them. As

Josephine grew older, she developed additional health problems, which began to affect her ability to perform.

JOSEPHINE'S FINAL PERFORMANCE

On April 8, 1975, when Josephine was sixty-eight years old, she opened in a show about

her life at a theater in Paris. It was her big comeback, and the reviews were stellar. She was magnificent!

That night, however, Josephine had a stroke while reading the reviews of her show. She was discovered the next day in a coma, surrounded by newspapers. She never regained consciousness, and four days later she died. Her funeral in Paris was a huge affair, with a twenty-one-gun military salute. She was the first American-born woman to merit such an honor. More than twenty thousand people lined the streets to pay their respects and say goodbye to the great Josephine Baker, diva and spy.

Unlike Josephine, who used her dazzling fame and extravagance to disarm and distract the enemy, smooth-talking crook Eddie Chapman used his cunning and sly charm to disguise his true intentions and help defeat the Nazis.

FOUR

Eddie Chapman
SAFECRACKER SPY

THE JELLY GANG

According to Eddie Chapman, it was easy to break open a safe. All you had to do was drill a hole in the lock and stuff some **gelignite** into the hole. Once you added a detonator, the gelignite would explode. The trick was not to use too much, or you might destroy the safe and all its contents—or blow yourself up.

Eddie learned this technique from his criminally minded pal James Hunt when he was just twenty years old. Together with another crook and a getaway driver, they went on a five-year safecracking and robbery spree in London, starting with a brazen theft of fur coats in 1934. They called themselves "the Jelly Gang," named for the jelly, or gelignite, which was a new discovery in London's safecracking underworld.

The Jelly Gang made Eddie a wealthy man, and he spent his money easily. It was a very different life from his tough childhood in the north of England. He'd dropped out of school at sixteen to make his own way. Now here he was, wearing expensive suits and driving a fancy car. He hung around in nightclubs, buying drinks for his new friends: gamblers, actors, journalists, diplomats, and high-rolling criminals like himself. One of his new friends was a film director named Terence Young, who later directed the first James Bond film. Eddie was having a grand time, and the police couldn't arrest him for his crimes. They had no evidence on him, and they'd never caught him in the act.

Eddie was charming and handsome, and he could talk

> **GELIGNITE** is an explosive material that was invented in 1875 and used mostly for demolition and mining. Spies—and criminals—found it handy for breaking into safes and blowing down locked doors.

to anybody about anything. He had lots of girlfriends, but the one he fell in love with was Betty. He told her he was in the film business. Of course everyone knew he was a crook, but they liked him anyway. Terence Young observed that Eddie "would steal the money from your pocket, even as he bought you a drink, but he never deserted a friend, nor hurt a soul."

In 1938 the police finally arrested Eddie for breaking into a store. He was granted bail. But when it came time for his trial, Eddie was nowhere to be found. He had skipped town.

EDDIE CHAPMAN (Agent Zigzag)

ON THE RUN

Eddie took Betty to Jersey, a self-governed nation in the Channel Islands between England and France. The couple hoped to travel from there to France, along with the rest of Eddie's gang, to avoid a prison sentence in England. They were having lunch when Eddie noticed a couple of men in overcoats and brown hats who had just entered the restaurant and were having a hushed talk with the headwaiter. They were undercover police detectives!

Eddie told Betty, "I shall go . . . but I shall always come back." He kissed her goodbye, jumped up from the table, crashed through a window, and ran off, followed by the police. It was the last Betty saw of him for six years.

A PRISON PLOT

The detectives caught Eddie, and the judge sentenced him to two years in prison. It's a good thing he was caught in Jersey, which had a separate legal system from the rest of the UK. If he had been caught in London, he would've been charged with all the additional crimes he'd committed—including jumping bail. In that case, he might have been sentenced to around fourteen years in prison, instead of just two years.

Even two years was tough on Eddie. Prison was boring. He later recalled that "the routine was monotonous; reading was the only relaxation. The library had about two hundred books, and before my time was half through I had read all of them." Naturally, Eddie tried to escape. When he was caught, his sentence was extended for another year. After that, he spent much of his prison sentence in solitary confinement.

That gave Eddie a lot of time to think about what he would do once he got out. He couldn't go back to London; the police were still looking for him there, and he would surely be arrested again. But England was his homeland, and he loved his country almost as much as he loved the thrill and adventure of being a crook.

Then the Germans invaded Jersey. And that gave Eddie an idea.

Eddie found foreign-language grammar books in the prison library and taught himself some French and German. As he did, he worked on his plan. In October 1941, when he finally got out of prison, Eddie went to the German command post in Jersey with a proposition.

"I would like to join the German secret service," he told them. There was nothing for him in England anymore, he explained. He revealed his history of thieving and safecracking, and told them that he was a wanted man in London. He said he admired the German spirit and would help them do anything that would damage Britain. He wanted his revenge.

Of course, he didn't really mean it. He figured he'd offer to spy for the Nazis, and then he'd bring all their secrets to Britain's secret service. He'd make himself so valuable to Britain that they'd drop all the criminal charges against him, and he'd be a free man. That was his plan.

But first he had to get himself into the Abwehr—the German secret service.

ARRESTED AGAIN

While Eddie was waiting to hear back from the Germans about his offer to spy for them, he started a black-market business, illegally buying and selling things that were hard to find in wartime. It wasn't long before the German military police found out what he was doing.

He was handcuffed and taken to a prison in France. This prison was much more interesting than the one in Jersey. For one thing, there were women there, in a separate section from the men. Naturally, Eddie figured out how to pick the locks on the doors that separated them, and they had some wild parties—until the guards discovered them. Eddie's charm kept him from being punished too severely. Even the prison guards liked him.

Meanwhile, the Abwehr hadn't forgotten about Eddie. One day, a German agent came to talk to him in the prison. She asked him a lot of questions. Eddie remembered them all. "What work did I think I could do in England? Was I prepared to carry out **sabotage**? Was it for money or for hatred of the British that I wanted to work against them? I told her that I was only interested in money and that I disliked the British, chiefly for their prisons and their police. I explained, as I had done before, that I was wanted by them on several criminal charges, and that if they ever caught up with me I would receive at least fifteen years."

> **SABOTAGE** is the deliberate destruction of property or equipment, usually done secretly. The word has French origins. It may possibly come from nineteenth-century France, when angry factory workers would throw their sabots (wooden clogs) into the machinery to keep it from functioning. During World War II, spies and other Resistance fighters frequently used sabotage to undermine the Axis powers.

GERMAN SPY SCHOOL

The next month, on April 10, 1942, Eddie was released from prison. He was escorted to a French chateau that had been taken over by the Abwehr as a training center for German spies. On the way there, he was taught to raise his right hand in the Nazi salute and say "Heil Hitler," a German phrase used as a greeting and sign of respect by Nazis and **Nazi sympathizers**.

At the chateau, Eddie was given lessons on how to be a spy. He was told never to speak English or French when he was outside of the chateau, only German. If anyone asked about his accent, he was supposed to say that he had been born in Germany, but had spent most of his life in the US.

> **NAZI SYMPATHIZERS** were people who agreed with Hitler's vision. But many Germans who considered themselves patriots—including some who worked for the government—privately disapproved of his agenda. Graumann was not the only Abwehr member who was anti-Hitler. Abwehr chief Admiral Wilhelm Canaris was loyal to his country and wanted Germany to win the war, but he was secretly opposed to the Nazis. In 1945, Hitler had him executed for treason.

Eddie's Abwehr handler was a distinguished-looking man named Doctor Graumann. Graumann took a great interest in Eddie, and taught him all about German culture. The two men got along very well. Although Graumann was German, he was neither a Nazi nor a Nazi sympathizer. He despised Hitler, but he was careful not to let anyone know this. Soon, though, he and Eddie were talking freely about politics. Graumann confided in Eddie, telling him that he thought the Nazis would end up destroying Germany. Fortunately, Eddie was a lot better at keeping secrets than Graumann was.

ADOLF HITLER salutes the Olympic flag at the opening of the Olympic Games in Berlin on August 1, 1936.

Eddie knew how to blow things up, but he had a lot to learn about sabotage, shooting a revolver, using Morse code, encoding and decoding messages, and working a radio transmitter. He got very good at sending Morse code messages and had his own unique style, or "**fist**." "I always ended with 'he, he, ha, ha' or some variation of laughing sounds," he said. He liked to fool around, and often included jokes in his practice messages.

His German spy name was Fritz. Soon he became known among the Abwehr ranks as Fritzchen, a friendly

FIST: Every wireless operator has his or her own particular way of sending a Morse code message. Their particular style is known as their "fist," and it is possible to identify an individual wireless operator by his or her fist. Noor Inayat Khan, the Sufi Princess Spy, was sometimes called "Bang Away Lulu" because of the way she banged at the lever.

nickname that indicated how much everyone liked him. But this well-liked fellow was thinking ahead—about how he would betray them once he got to England.

Eddie eavesdropped on the Nazis and took notes about code words and radio transmissions. He snooped around and memorized the chemical formulas for bombs. Bit by bit, he amassed secrets that he hoped would one day find their way to British Intelligence.

A BOMBING MISSION

In June 1942, Eddie received orders for his first mission: parachute into England and blow up an airplane factory. The de Havilland plant manufactured Mosquito bombers, which were doing great damage to the Nazis. Eddie was also told to report back on whatever other information might be helpful to the Abwehr. He would be paid 100,000 reichsmarks, which was the German currency at the time—approximately equivalent to $40,000 today—and when he returned, he would get even more money.

"If caught, I was not to divulge that I was employed by the German government nor mention any of the names of the German personnel with whom I had been trained. . . . The penalty for divulging any of this information, or betraying the German Reich, was death." In fact, if he was caught, he had orders to pretend to offer his services to the British secret service, and make sure to get sent back to France, where he could report back to the Abwehr as a **triple agent**.

In preparation for his mission, Eddie took parachuting lessons and learned to write in invisible ink using a specially prepared matchstick treated with secret ink. He also had to get rid of anything that might identify him as a German spy, so the Abwehr found him British clothing and gave him false British papers with a fake name.

Eddie was also given a **bluff check**, in case he was captured. If he included "FFFFF" in his messages, they would know everything was all right. If it wasn't there, it would mean he had been caught, and someone else was sending the message, pretending to be him.

While a double agent is a spy who is working for one side while pretending to work for the other, a TRIPLE AGENT pretends to be a double agent for one side, but is actually a double agent for the other side.

It wasn't until November that he was finally given the okay to carry out his mission. As he got ready to leave, Eddie collected all the information he had about his German handler and the spy center. He wrote everything down in a little notebook: names, dates, places, formulas, codes—anything he had seen or heard that might help the Allies. He would tape the notebook to his body, under his clothing, so nobody would see it. He planned to hand it over to the British secret service.

Then, the night before he left, Graumann told him that he was going to be thoroughly searched, to make sure there wasn't anything in his clothing or on his person that might identify him as a German spy. In a panic, Eddie tore up his notes and flushed them down the toilet. He'd just have to remember it all.

> A BLUFF CHECK is a security measure for spies, a way of sending a secret signal hidden in a wireless message. Each operator has a unique bluff check.

BRITISH CODE BREAKERS HEAR EVERYTHING

In 1940, code breakers at **Bletchley Park** in England had finally broken the German **Enigma Machine's** encrypted messages, which had once been thought to be unbreakable. Secret messages being transmitted from Germany were no longer secret, because the British could now intercept and decode all German communications. They gave this operation the code name Ultra. The material Ultra produced was called the "Most Secret Sources." It was crucial that the Germans never find out that the British could read all of their messages. This was one of the most important secrets of the war.

In 1942, the code breakers were listening in when the Germans started reporting on their British agent Fritzchen. He sounded like an important spy. But Fritzchen's own messages were baffling, with his joking manner and odd references. For instance, Fritzchen sent a cryptic message about Bobby the Pig, who was growing fatter every day. Who was Bobby the Pig? Was he a Nazi? And what did it mean that he was growing fatter?

Eddie was actually writing about a pet pig he had gotten while he was in Germany. He'd named it Bobby, using the British slang term for a police officer. He thought it was funny

BLETCHLEY PARK is a nineteenth-century British mansion and estate that was transformed into a top-secret code-breaking and intelligence center in 1938. Located in the countryside beyond London, Bletchley Park was hidden from the public. It played an enormous role in winning the war.

Thousands of people worked as code breakers at or around Bletchley Park during the war. They included mathematicians and linguists, clerical workers and university students, service members and civilians. More than half of them were women. Some were invited there after winning crossword puzzle competitions; the kind of thinking that made someone good at crossword puzzles was the kind of thinking that would also make them good at breaking codes.

The most famous person at Bletchley Park was mathematician Alan Turing. He invented a machine called the Bombe that helped decipher messages.

The people who worked at Bletchley Park were forbidden to talk about what they did—even after the war had ended. British Prime Minister Winston Churchill called them "the geese that laid the golden eggs and never cackled," in reference to the code breakers and their success in keeping their work secret. In 2014, a restoration of Bletchley Park was completed. It is open to the public as a museum where you can see the code breakers' huts and some of the machines, and learn about the history of this fascinating place and the people who worked there.

that his devoted pet followed him around everywhere, just like the police used to do when he was a crook.

Any messages to do with Fritzchen got the British secret service's immediate attention. Before long, they learned that Fritzchen had been assigned to spy for the Germans in England, and to carry out an act of sabotage. But who was this Fritzchen? When was he coming? What was his target? They hoped they would be able to find him when he finally did land in England, so that they could keep him from blowing anything up. Maybe they could turn him into a double agent.

SWAPPING SIDES

Early in the morning of December 16, 1942, Eddie was flown to England. He hadn't put on his oxygen mask properly, so he got a nosebleed from the altitude. His stomach flip-flopped with nausea as the plane swooped. When he tried to jump, his backpack got caught in the hatchway and he hung there in midair until someone gave him a shove and pushed him through the opening.

He parachuted onto British soil, landing in a celery field. He had lost his map, and he was miles away from the place where he was supposed to be. He wandered around in a daze until he found a farmhouse. He knocked on the door and said that he was a British airman flying in from France. He said his plane had developed engine trouble.

After a cup of tea, he asked to use the phone, and he called the local police department. When the police arrived, he handed them his pistol and told them that he wouldn't answer any of their questions. He wanted to talk to the British intelligence service.

He was taken to the police station, where he was searched. They found the suicide pill he had hidden in the cuff of his pants. He told them about his flight, and a little about his time in prison. But he wouldn't say more, only that he had an interesting story that he would tell only to someone in British Intelligence.

AGENT ZIGZAG

British Intelligence came to get Eddie. Perhaps he could be this Fritzchen they were looking for— the British spy whom the Germans were planning to send to England to spy on them. They took him to a former prison in London that was being used for top-secret interrogations.

They questioned Eddie for two days. They

The ENIGMA MACHINE was used by the Germans to encipher messages. It had three levels of settings for each letter, making it nearly impossible to decipher the message unless you knew what the settings were. Another cipher machine was called the Lorenz. At Bletchley Park, the code breakers figured out how to break those ciphers, by using special machines, like the one invented by Alan Turing. Without the machines, they could never have figured it out.

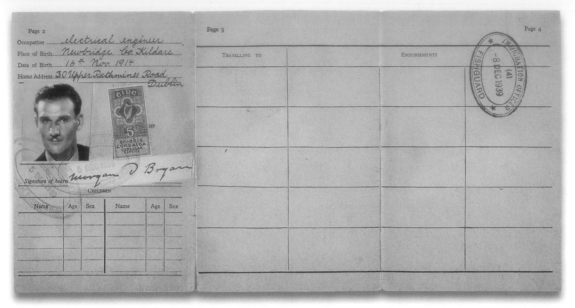

EDDIE CHAPMAN'S false Irish passport

wanted to find out if he was really Fritzchen, as he claimed, and if he was telling them the truth about wanting to help them. He told them everything he knew about the Abwehr and his experience there, all the information he could remember from the notes he had destroyed.

They looked over the equipment he had brought with him: his wireless transmitter, his suicide pill, his special matches for writing secret messages. They examined every piece of paper in his wallet. It was all fake, Eddie told them, except for one item: a letter from his girlfriend, Betty.

The British secret service decided that Eddie was telling them the truth. He was definitely the German agent Fritzchen, and he would make a valuable double agent. He would have to be watched, of course. After all, he was a crook. And he would have to lie low to avoid getting arrested by the British police. They couldn't tell anyone that he was in the secret service—not even the police—so they wouldn't be able to help him if he were arrested. He'd just have to be very careful and not get himself arrested again.

His interrogators wrote, "In our opinion, Chapman should be used to the fullest extent. . . . He genuinely means to work for the British against the Germans. By his courage and resourcefulness he is ideally fitted to be an agent." They gave him the code name Zigzag, and he became part of the **Double Cross** team, composed of all the German agents who had become double agents working for British Intelligence.

Then Agent Zigzag sent his first message as a British double agent. He started off with his bluff check: FFFFF. "Well. Am with friends. Good landing. Fritz." He ended the message with a variation of his laughing sign-off. The British code breakers listened in to see what the Germans would say about his message. They overheard various transmissions from the Abwehr saying that they were glad to know he had arrived safely and that they were certain it was really him, because they recognized his style and sign-off.

Now he would have to fulfill his mission before the Abwehr suspected otherwise.

As the Germans tried to build a spy network in England, the British worked equally hard to destroy it. According to MI5, every single German spy sent over to Britain was caught and either turned into a double agent or imprisoned and/or executed. British Major John Masterman and Colonel Tommy Robertson were in charge of the committee that ran these double agents, nicknamed DOUBLE CROSS. The Germans never found out. Throughout the war, they believed that their spy network was providing important information. However, all of that information was controlled by MI5 to help the Allies win the war. This included some less important nuggets of true information (known as "chicken feed") mixed in with lots of false information (known as "disinformation") to get the Germans to believe whatever MI5 wanted them to believe.

"BLOWING UP" A FACTORY

Eddie's mission as Fritz was to blow up the de Havilland airplane factory. But his mission as Agent Zigzag was *not* to blow up the factory, and to trick the Germans into thinking he had. How could he possibly do both?

With the help of MI5 and the Double Cross team, he came up with a plan. He would use camouflage and trickery to make it look like part of the factory had been blown up. The Germans would be flying overhead later to see if he had been successful, so he would have to make it look real from above. But he would also have to hide it from passersby, who could see it at ground level. He would have to do all this without alerting the public that anything was going on. And he didn't want the factory workers to suspect anything, either.

R.A.F. day raiders over Berlin's official quarter.

BACK THEM UP!

PRINTED FOR H.M. STATIONERY OFFICE BY FOSH & CROSS LTD., LONDON. 51-2395

This British poster shows a de Havilland Mosquito bomber dropping bombs on Berlin.

First he scoped out the factory. He broke in one night and took a look around. He found just what he was looking for: there was an abandoned swimming pool in a walled-in area behind a locked gate, as well as the boiler and pump that had been used for the pool. The Germans had no idea about the swimming pool. According to the data they had given him, they believed that there were transformers there, and that they were an important part of the factory. Nobody from the factory went in there anymore. In fact, it was hidden from view of anyone in the building. It would be the perfect target.

The next step was to go shopping for the materials he would need to make the bombs. They had to be things easily found in war-torn Britain, in order to convince the Abwehr. Of course, he didn't actually make any bombs. It was all part of the trick.

Magician Spy Jasper Maskelyne was consulted to help create the illusion, to make it "look, from the air, as if the place had been blown to Kingdom Come." They constructed papier-mâché and wood replicas of some of the machinery. These would be rolled onto their sides to look as though they had been knocked over by the blast. Then they painted netting and iron sheets to look like a big hole in the ground, as if it had been made by a bomb blast. That would disguise the real machinery. They built fake broken gates and painted tarps to look like the remains of a blasted brick wall. They also gathered extra debris to spread around. And on a cloudy night, they broke in and staged their deception.

MI5 realized that an explosion at an important factory would surely be reported in the British newspapers. So they found a way to plant a fake article about a factory explosion in the *Daily Express*. The article appeared the next day, February 1, 1943.

The Germans flew overhead a few days later and saw the "destruction." They were very pleased with Fritzchen's sabotage, and sent him a message of congratulations. Later that year, they awarded him the Iron Cross for bravery in his work on behalf of the Abwehr. The Iron Cross was a high German honor, and Eddie was the only British citizen who ever received this "prestigious" medal.

SPY TRICKS

Eddie's next assignment as Zigzag was to return to France and start spying on the Germans. Before he left, he met with Victor, Lord Rothschild. Rothschild was a British millionaire and scientist.

He was also head of MI5's explosives and sabotage section. His job was to keep Britain safe from sabotage, and included everything from defusing German bombs to making sure that Prime Minister Winston Churchill's cigars hadn't been booby-trapped. Rothschild taught Eddie how to make a piece of coal into a bomb, and Eddie taught Rothschild how to crack open a safe using gelignite. The two of them got along very well!

British Prime Minister **WINSTON CHURCHILL** visits the American ambassador at the US embassy in London on May 9, 1945, the day after the German surrender. He's giving the famous "V for victory" sign.

Before Eddie left for France, Rothschild asked him to bring back some German equipment for Rothschild to study: bombs, detonators, whatever else Eddie could find.

The plan was for Eddie to join the crew of a British ship heading to Lisbon. He had a fake name and he was disguised as a seaman. The only person who knew he was in disguise was the ship's captain, and he was sworn to secrecy. Once Eddie was in Lisbon, he'd meet up with Abwehr members, who would take him back to France.

MI5 figured out a tricky way for Eddie to send them messages, hidden in his messages to the Abwehr. He would use variations of his laughing sign-off. Each variation had a different meaning. For instance, "Hu hu hu" meant that he had no information for them. "Hi ha hu" meant he was going to Berlin. "He he he" meant he was going to America. He could speak to MI5 right under the noses of the Abwehr, and they would have no idea.

When the ship docked in Lisbon, Eddie had another idea. He told the Abwehr that he wanted to blow up the British ship for them. He told them he had learned how to make a piece of coal into a bomb. He described it to them, and said that they should make the bomb for him. Then he'd hide it in with the coal on the ship. It wouldn't go off until it was shoveled into the boiler, when the ship was out at sea again. Then it would blow the ship sky high.

The Germans were thrilled. They made the bomb for Eddie per his description, but used their ingenuity to build their own version of it. It was a perfect piece of German engineering.

Eddie's plan was a brilliant one. For one thing, his idea to blow up a British ship would convince the Germans that he was still on their side. Of course, he wouldn't actually plant the bomb on the ship. He talked with the captain, and then MI5 helped him find a way to make some smoke and noise on the ship once it was at sea, without blowing it up. He would tell the Germans that their bomb must have malfunctioned.

For another thing, this German version of the coal bomb might reveal something important about their scientific methods and materials. Eddie contacted an MI5 colleague and gave him the German coal bomb, with instructions to deliver it—carefully—to Rothschild. Wouldn't he be pleased to have another German bomb to examine!

BACK TO BRITAIN—
AS A TRIPLE AGENT?

The ENIGMA MACHINE, invented in 1923, was used by the Germans during World War II to encipher and decipher messages. When the British at Bletchley Park broke the Enigma cipher, it was a major factor in winning the war.

Eddie was given his next mission as Fritz in 1944. Germany was losing the battle with Britain at sea. Eddie's orders were to find out why. The true reason was that the British were now deciphering the Enigma code. They knew where every German battleship and submarine could be found—and attacked. But the Germans didn't know that. And neither did Eddie. (Even spies didn't know all the secrets.) As before, Eddie was also commanded to find out anything else that would help the Germans.

So Eddie parachuted into Britain a second time. He later recalled, "I pulled the lever, and the door beneath me dropped away. . . . I dropped clear of the plane, which spun off into the darkness. A short drop—*zack*—my chute was open! I swung in the empty sky, like a pendulum in a vast clock. It was too much for my rebellious stomach. I leaned over the side of my harness and spewed over England."

He found his way to London and made contact with MI5. Then he gave them all of the information he'd collected while in France. After MI5 had finished questioning and examining him, they determined that he was, indeed, still loyal to Britain. His information was legitimate. He hadn't become a triple agent. Then he was allowed to send a message to Graumann: "Safe. FFFFF. Will contact in seven days."

One of Eddie's next tasks as Fritz was to let the Nazis know about the exact effects of their V-1 bombs. These unmanned flying bombs were also known as doodlebugs or buzz bombs,

London, 1944. This man took his dog for a walk and returned to a scene of devastation: his home had been destroyed in a V-1 bomb attack. The policeman is offering tea and sympathy. In the background, rescue workers are searching for survivors. This entire street was destroyed in the attack, but the man and his dog survived.

because of the buzzing sound they made. Where did they land? How much damage did they cause? The Germans wanted the bombs to land right in central London, to do the most damage possible. Eddie's information would help them to figure out if they were aiming the bombs correctly, so they could send more bombs and do even greater damage.

MI5 helped Eddie figure out what to tell them, to make sure that the German bombs actually landed *away* from the most highly populated parts of London. That way, fewer people would be killed. Eddie had to be very careful, however. If he directed them too far away, the Germans would find out and they'd be suspicious. So the calculations had to be just right. Another British double agent, code-named Garbo—the Storyteller Spy also known as Juan Pujol Garcia—provided information to the Nazis, as well, that confirmed whatever Eddie told the Abwehr. Between the two spies, and with help from MI5, they saved many people's lives.

In November 1944, MI5 decided it was time to dismiss Eddie. Although he'd done a tremendous amount to help them in the fight against the Nazis, he was still a crook, and he had a tendency to brag. They were worried that he might give away important information. So they had him sign the **Official Secrets Act**. And then they fired him.

I'LL ALWAYS COME BACK

The OFFICIAL SECRETS ACT was used to keep British spies from spilling the beans about their work in the secret service. It was binding even after they had left their secret service employment. It said, in part, "I undertake not to divulge any official information gained by me as a result of my employment, either in the press or in book form." It threatened anyone who was guilty of doing so with a prison sentence and a fine.

After the war, Eddie wanted to find Betty, the love of his life. He didn't know where she was, and he had no idea where to start looking. He asked two of his former MI5 contacts to help him. They met at a restaurant in a fancy London hotel to come up with a plan.

The agents said that if Eddie wanted them to find her, they'd need to know what she looked like. Eddie looked around and pointed to a blond-haired woman at a table across the room, who had her back to them. He commented that the woman looked exactly like Betty from the back. Then the woman turned around.

It was Betty!

AN EXCITING STORY TO TELL

Eddie and Betty got married, and they had a daughter. Eddie's police record had been cleared, as a reward for his service for MI5. As a double agent, he'd had quite an education. He'd learned various skills, including photography and sailing, and he'd learned French, German, Norwegian, and some Dutch.

But his spying had also taught him some useful new criminal skills. Before long, Eddie returned to a life of crime. He became a gold smuggler and hung around with crooks. He had quite a lot of money from his intelligence work, and he took to wearing fancy clothes again and

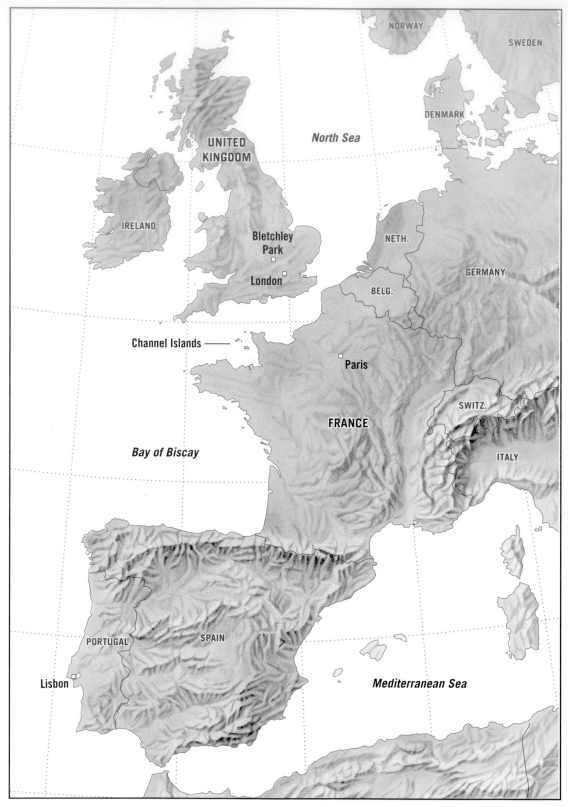

Western Europe, where **EDDIE CHAPMAN** used his criminal know-how against the Nazis

driving around in a big Rolls-Royce. He even became the crime correspondent for a British newspaper.

Eddie knew that he himself had an exciting story to tell, and he wanted the world to know. He wrote some articles about his adventures, and they were published in a French newspaper in 1953. Then he wrote a memoir, with the help of a British journalist named Frank Owen. But the British War Office stopped publication of the book, citing the Official Secrets Act. When Eddie complained, they threatened to throw him in prison.

The Eddie Chapman Story, under the byline of Frank Owen, was published at last in 1954. MI5 had forced Eddie to remove every reference to his work for the British secret service. He wasn't terribly happy about that, because it made him look like a traitor. But he had no choice.

Years later, in 1966, Eddie was finally allowed to publish *The Real Eddie Chapman Story.* It was nearly identical to the first book, and he still wasn't allowed to write about his British spy work. However, this book included chapters written by another journalist, which summarized Eddie's work for MI5 and details about how he did it. Since the journalist hadn't signed the Official Secrets Act, he was free to tell Eddie's story for him. Finally the world learned that Eddie wasn't just a crook, but a British spy and war hero, too.

Eddie died in 1997 at the age of eighty-three.

Eddie used his charisma to charm the world, and bragged about his exploits. Another spy, Virginia Hall, used her strength of character to overcome tremendous obstacles, and fought the Nazis without fanfare.

FIVE

Virginia Hall
MOST-WANTED SPY

MIDNIGHT PARACHUTE DROP

The small plane flew low in the still night, over the farms and forests of rural France. A coded radio message, "The robin sings in the morning," had already been sent to tell the **Maquis** where and when the plane would arrive. Now the pilot was sending a radio transmission giving the password, and the Maquis leader on the other end replied in a coded response: "It's safe."

The plane circled down toward a field, guided through the dark by a line of torches. It never touched down. At the last moment before it sped off again, a parachute was released over the field, bearing a large metal container. Inside were boxes with guns and ammunition, some American cigarettes, cans of maple syrup, and a small package marked "Diane."

Waiting at the edge of the field, men and women rushed in to take away the prizes. Later, the parachute silk would be given to the local women to sew into clothing. The guns and ammunition would be distributed to the Maquis, along with the cigarettes and maple syrup. And

The MAQUIS were a scrappy, renegade part of the French Resistance. They lived in the mountainous regions of France, often camping out in the hills and living rough. *Maquis* is the French word for a special kind of underbrush that grows in the scrubby wilderness areas of that part of the countryside. Many of the Maquis were fugitives from forced labor; the Nazis required all young Frenchmen to go to Germany to work for the Nazi empire.

Members of the Maquis were divided into small groups, called cells, each led by a different person. They only knew the people in their cell. That way, if they were caught, they would only be able to identify their cell members, but would not be in a position to endanger the rest of the Maquis.

Maquis parachutes landing in Villelonge, France
(near Le Chambon-sur-Lignon)

the small package? A box of British tea, flown in specially for the Maquis leader of the region:
Virginia Hall, code name Diane.

STRONG-WILLED AND FEISTY

Virginia was born in Maryland, where she and her brother grew up hunting and riding horseback. She was smart and athletic and strong-willed, as well. Her parents sent her to the best schools, and she studied hard and traveled throughout Europe. She began college at Barnard and Radcliffe, then transferred to the Sorbonne in France, and then attended the Konsularakademie in Vienna. Quick with languages, she became fluent in German, Italian, and French (although she never lost her American accent), and picked up some Polish and Russian.

After graduation, Virginia got a job at the State Department and was stationed at the American consulate in Turkey. One day, when she was hunting grouse, she slipped in the mud. *Boom!* Her gun went off by accident, and she shot herself in the foot. Shot at such close range, her foot was completely destroyed. It took so long to get her to a hospital that she developed gangrene. The entire bottom half of her left leg had to be amputated, just below her knee.

But Virginia was moving again in no time, wooden leg and all. She found a way to take long strides, which made her limp less noticeable, and she gave her wooden leg a name: Cuthbert. When Poland was invaded by Germany in 1939, Virginia and Cuthbert went off to France to

The OFFICE OF STRATEGIC SERVICES (OSS) was the American intelligence service during World War II, and was a predecessor of the CIA (Central Intelligence Agency). William J. Donovan, a special advisor to President Franklin D. Roosevelt, was asked by the president to create the wartime agency based on the British Secret Intelligence Service (MI6) and Special Operations Executive (SOE). The previous US spying agency had been shut down in 1929 because, according to the then secretary of state, Henry Stimson, "gentlemen don't read each other's mail."

The OSS was responsible for coordinating espionage activities outside of the US. Among its many duties and missions, the OSS recruited and trained spies, collected information, spread disinformation, oversaw distribution of anti-Nazi propaganda, and organized anti-Nazi resistance. The OSS helped to arm the French Resistance, arranging for secret shipments of weapons and ammunition along with other necessities to wage war against the Nazis.

help the Allied war effort by driving an ambulance. There she began to witness the horrors of war first-hand, and she was appalled by what she saw.

In 1940, when the Nazis took over France, Virginia determined to find a way of using her language skills and her incredible stamina to help fight the Nazis. She applied to join the **Office of Strategic Services**, the US government organization in charge of espionage activities outside of the country. She knew how adaptable and capable she was. There was just one problem: the OSS wouldn't hire anyone with a false limb.

Virginia wasn't the type to sit around and mope. Instead, off she went to London to see what she could do there. Before long, she was recruited by Britain's top-secret **Special Operations Executive**. The SOE was in charge of spying and resistance activities in Nazi-occupied Europe. They didn't care whether Virginia had a wooden leg or not.

AN "OLD" LADY AND HER NETWORK OF SPIES

Because Virginia's French was fluent, the SOE decided to send her to France. She was the first female SOE agent to be stationed there. Before she departed, the SOE trained her in weapons, encoding and decoding secret messages, map reading, establishing security measures, and monitoring Resistance activities. The only thing she couldn't do was a parachute jump, because of Cuthbert. So the SOE shipped her to France by boat to set up a secret Resistance network, all while maintaining a fairly visible day job.

VIRGINIA HALL

Virginia had written some articles for her college newspaper. That experience, along with a discreet letter of recommendation from the SOE, got her a job writing as a foreign correspondent for the *New York Post*. Under cover as an American journalist, Virginia filed reports and articles from Vichy, France, that contained coded information about what was happening in the country.

When Virginia's contact at the SOE told her to move from Vichy to Lyon, she put on a disguise. Even though they were on the lookout for spies, the Nazis didn't notice the disheveled old lady hobbling from the train to her destination. Nobody would suspect that she was a spy, carrying lots of money for the Resistance stuffed under her clothing.

Before long, Virginia became the number-one contact person for many of the French Resistance members in the region. Besides putting them in touch with other Resistance members and equipping them with money, fake identification cards, and radio transmitters, she also recruited new Resistance members. She helped save the lives of escaped prisoners of war and stranded pilots by passing them along to others who would help them flee.

The **SPECIAL OPERATIONS EXECUTIVE (SOE)**, founded at the request of England's Prime Minister Winston Churchill, was the British secret service during World War II. Churchill wanted the SOE to "set Europe ablaze." In operation from July 1940 through January 1946, the SOE was in charge of spying and sabotage in occupied Europe, and aided the Resistance in the fight against the Nazis. There were stations of the SOE in other parts of the world, including a branch office in New York City, which coordinated with the OSS and the FBI.

MOST-WANTED: *LA DAME QUI BOITE*

The Nazis in and around Lyon eventually figured out that there was a spy in the region who had a tremendous amount of power. French double

DISGUISES

This packet contains FALSE WHISKERS, EYEBROWS ETC. & ADHESIVE TAPE FOR ATTACHING THESE TO FACE.

Disguise yourself as illustrated!

False facial hair was not a disguise worn by VIRGINIA HALL, but WWII-era disguise kits such as this offered options to people who wanted to conceal their identities.

agents had described her to the Nazis, calling her "*la dame qui boite*" ("the limping lady"). Virginia was up at the top of the **Gestapo**'s most-wanted list.

Although they knew a little about her, they weren't sure exactly who or where she was. They desperately wanted to find her, to stop her from doing any more damage. If they found her, they would arrest and interrogate her, most likely using torture, before killing her.

GESTAPO is short for *Geheime Staatspolizei*, the Nazi state secret police. They were particularly brutal, and were responsible for arresting and torturing many thousands of people.

Finally, in November 1942, it became too dangerous for Virginia to stay in France. There were rumors that the Nazis would be arriving in Lyon the next day to search for her. She had to escape. She caught the last train that night, heading toward the border with Spain. From Spain, she would have to make her way back to London. For part of the journey, she had to travel on foot across the Pyrenees mountains. It was hard going, especially with her wooden leg. She had terrible blisters on the stump of her leg, but she refused to let them stop her. At one point during her arduous journey, she was able to send a radio message to the SOE in England:

"Cuthbert is being tiresome, but I can cope."

The reply was:

"If Cuthbert tiresome, have him eliminated."

Clearly, they had forgotten who Cuthbert was!

PLAYING THE PIANO AND PLAYING A MILKMAID

Once she arrived in London, Virginia convinced the SOE to train her as a "piano player"—the code word for a wireless operator, someone who knew how to transmit and receive coded messages by radio transmitter. Now she would be able to send her own secret messages. However, transmitting these messages was an extremely dangerous job. If the Nazis picked up a radio transmission, they could quickly find the source. They'd rush in and arrest the wireless operator, sometimes even catching them while they were still transmitting.

By 1944, the SOE was working closely with the OSS in the fight against the Nazis. Virginia was able to transfer to the OSS, because of her valuable experience in France. So it was as a member of the OSS that Virginia returned to France, to a region in south-central France called the Haute-Loire.

At first, she continued to use her cover as an American journalist. This gave her access to many different people. When she interviewed them for the articles she was writing, she was able to learn about the surroundings and get messages out to the local Resistance groups.

She ended up in a village called Le Chambon-sur-Lignon, a hardscrabble farming community on a mountain plateau. One day she approached August Bohny, the guardian of a children's

View of Le Chambon-sur-Lignon, France, during World War II

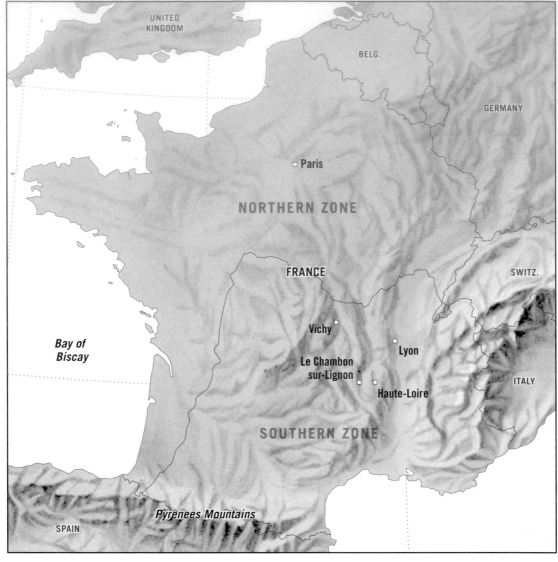

VIRGINIA HALL was stationed throughout France as she aided the Resistance during WWII.

home run by the Swiss Red Cross. She told him she was writing an article about Swiss Aid for Children. As they talked, she mentioned that she was interested in learning about the Maquis.

Bohny told her that he couldn't help her. But he understood that she wanted him to put her in touch with the Maquis, so that she could help *them*. He knew that some of the counselors at the Swiss Aid homes had close ties to the Maquis, so he decided to tell them about the journalist. Then they did exactly what he'd hoped they would: they went to their friends in the Maquis and told them to contact Virginia. She had a radio transmitter, which would enable them to communicate with other Resistance members and get information about weapons caches, dead drops, and so on. She could also provide other badly needed supplies, such as ammunition, medical supplies, food, clothing, more radio transmitters, and money. After the war, Bohny said, "I received a letter of gratitude from one of the heads of the Maquis who wrote that if I had not responded the way I did in 1944, the 850 Maquis of the Haute-Loire would not have had weapons."

Once she had established contact with the Maquis, Virginia put on another disguise. She became a milkmaid and found a place to live on a farm. This disguise allowed her to search the countryside for good places for parachute drops from the supply planes. Outsiders saw a shabby old French milkmaid walking along the roads and fields with her cows. But some of the locals, who knew better, called her "the English lady."

The family that owned the farm where she lived were cheese-makers. Virginia decided that she would learn how to make cheese. Then she could go to the market to sell it. The German soldiers shopping there didn't know that she could understand German. They didn't realize that the French cheese seller was eavesdropping on them, and reporting everything they said back to her handlers in London.

The MAQUIS in Le Chambon-sur-Lignon, France

VIRGINIA IN CHARGE: *THE DAISIES WILL BLOOM TONIGHT*

Virginia became the leader of a cell of six Resistance fighters in the Maquis. Eventually she was in charge of nearly 1,500 men and women who were all anxious to defeat Hitler and help to free France from Nazi rule. Her main job was to coordinate the parachute drops, which were crucial for getting supplies from England to the Resistance. She set up a radio transmitter

THE DAISIES WILL BLOOM TONIGHT is the title of a painting commemorating Virginia Hall and her bravery. The title refers to one of the coded messages she received, giving information about a parachute drop of supplies. The painting depicts Virginia transmitting a message in the hayloft of a barn in Le Chambon. Shown with her is Edmond Lebrat, one of her captains, pedaling the bicycle to generate power for the radio transmitter. The painting, done many years later, is based partly on information from Lebrat's cousin, who was a child at the time and remembered seeing Virginia and Edmond when they were transmitting messages.

in the barn of the farm where she lived. Someone would have to pedal a modified bicycle to generate power to keep it running. This radio transmitter was precious. With it, Virginia could be directly in touch with the outside world, with her spy handler. But if it were discovered, she would be thrown into prison—or worse.

One of the men who worked in her cell said, "It was dangerous. People were often caught by the Germans and shot dead. . . . They could very easily have attacked us in the night, as we waited for parachute drops of supplies and agents. It was dark and we were all there. There might be traitors who knew the password that Diane or the Resistance head would use. For example, 'A robin sings in the morning' meant that there would be a parachute drop at such and such a place and time. When the plane came from London or Algiers, the pilot would radio Diane with the password, and she would reply with a coded message so that the pilot would know it was really her and it was safe. They had to be careful because sometimes, after they had arrested someone from the Resistance, or talked to a traitor, the Germans would know where the parachute drop was going to be. Or they might divert the pilot by directing him to a false location. And then the German soldiers would seize the containers as they landed, taking everything."

Often, new SOE or OSS members were flown in to help Virginia and the Resistance. They were all trained in parachuting, but the landings didn't always go smoothly. Sometimes the parachutists missed their mark and had to quickly hide their parachutes and find their way to the landing field on foot. Sometimes they landed badly and suffered broken bones. One time, an

SOE member from Scotland, who was wearing a kilt, parachuted in, but he landed in a tree and was stuck there. Fortunately Virginia and her men found him before the Germans did.

For safety, Virginia moved again, to another farm. This time she was disguised as a goatherd, which gave her the same opportunity to roam the fields in search of good landing strips for supply planes. She also trained the Maquis in using explosives to sabotage the Nazis by blowing up bridges and train tracks.

It was September 1944, and two new men from the US had recently parachuted in to work with her. One of them, Paul Goillot, was French. His family had moved to the US when he was a teenager. He and Virginia hit it off immediately. He made her laugh. She had tried never to become too close to anyone she worked with in the Resistance, but she made an exception for Paul.

EXTREME GALLANTRY

Virginia worked tirelessly for the OSS and the Maquis until the end of the war. After that, Virginia and Paul remained in France for a while, traveling to all of Virginia's old haunts to see how her contacts had fared. She also tried to retrieve all the hidden radio transmitters she'd left behind, so that she could bring them back to London.

In May 1945, Virginia was awarded the Distinguished Service Cross by the president of the

The Maquis preparing an explosive device at Le Chambon-sur-Lignon, France

Les Marguerites Fleuriront ce Soir (*The Daisies Will Bloom Tonight*) by Jeffrey W. Bass, CIA Intelligence Art Collection

United States. This award is given for "extreme gallantry and risk of life in actual combat with an armed enemy force." Virginia was the only civilian woman in World War II to receive the award. She asked that it be given in a private ceremony, as she still hoped to work undercover. However, in 1946 the OSS ceased operation.

In 1948 Virginia joined the CIA, where she was asked to prepare reports. She preferred to work in the field as an agent, but the CIA didn't agree. Despite all she had done during World War II, they didn't think it was a suitable job for a woman.

SPIES LIVE HAPPILY EVER AFTER

In 1950, Virginia and Paul were married. She was forty-four years old. When she retired from the CIA in 1966, they moved to a farm in Maryland, and she spent the rest of her life gardening, raising poodles, and doing crossword puzzles. She also took up cheese-making again. She died on July 12, 1982, and Paul died in 1987.

Virginia was able to make a life for herself after the war, and lived happily into old age. Not everyone battling the Nazis was so lucky. One of them was Noor Inayat Khan, a Sufi princess and a courageous spy to the end.

SIX

Noor Inayat Khan
SUFI PRINCESS SPY

LIBERTÉ!

For hours, the Nazi officer had tortured and beaten her. Now the young woman lay motionless on the ground, bloody and battered.

The officer shouted at her to get up onto her knees.

She slowly, painfully raised herself up. He held a pistol to her head.

Right before he fired, she spoke at last, just one word: "*Liberté!*"

THE CHARMED CHILDHOOD OF A SUFI PRINCESS

You'd never guess from Noor Inayat Khan's childhood that she would grow up to be a courageous spy. True, she was a descendant of the "Tiger of Mysore," a fierce emperor back in eighteenth-century India. But her father was a kind **Sufi** teacher, a talented musician, and a pacifist. He had left India to teach the Western world about Indian music and Sufism.

Her mother was an American. Noor's parents met in New York, then traveled to Russia, where Noor was born in 1914. Her full first name was Noor-un-nisa, which means "Light of womanhood" in Urdu, but everyone in her family called her Babuly ("Father's daughter").

Noor's family moved to London, and then to France, and Noor soon had two brothers and a sister. Their home in Paris, Fazal Manzil—the House of Blessing—became a center for Sufi teaching and music. It wasn't just for Sufis. People of all faiths came to study with Noor's father, to share ideas, and to listen to music.

A SUFI is a follower of Sufism. Sufism is a mystical and spiritual form of Islam. Sufis seek to open their hearts to find a personal, spiritual, direct connection with God through meditation, introspection, and prayer. Noor's family practiced tolerance and were pacifists, meaning they opposed the use of violence to settle disputes. The thirteenth-century Iranian poet Rumi was a Sufi.

Noor and her siblings were very close. They had a charmed life and they were loved and cherished. Their father sang them to sleep each night and woke them each morning with sacred Sufi songs, and he taught them about Sufi spirituality. They learned to respect and honor life. Each of them played several musical instruments. Noor's favorite was the harp.

She was a small, dreamy child, full of compassion. She was always adopting injured animals to care for them. "She lived in a magical world, surrounded by enchantment and beneficent beings," her nephew Pir Zia Inayat Khan said. Her close friend Jean Overton Fuller recalled, "There was something elfin about her." Her voice was "the thinnest little pipe—aerial as a bat's squeak—such a voice as creatures out of fairyland might be expected to use."

Noor had a vivid imagination. She claimed she could see fairies, and she loved making up stories about small creatures. When she was four, Noor made up a little song:

Do you like mice?

I like mice.

Do you like them in the house or in the garden?

If you don't like them in the house,

Pick them up and put them in the garden.

As she grew older, she began writing down her stories, and she painted sweet illustrations to go with them. She also wrote poems for her family members on their birthdays. When she was twelve, she composed a poem for a friend's birthday that included the lines:

What do you say, pretty stream,

In this valley peaceful and sweet?

I listen to the song of the water;

Which runs from its source to the end.

She decided that she would be a children's book writer when she grew up.

TAKING CARE OF EVERYBODY

When Noor was thirteen, her beloved father died. Everyone was in shock. Her mother went into a deep depression. Suddenly, Noor was in charge. As the oldest child,
she felt that she had to take care of the family and the
entire household.

She worked hard, and she also went to school and
took music lessons. Her life was very busy. After a few
years, her mother began to recover. But Noor always felt
a responsibility to care for her mother and protect her.

As Noor grew older, she studied child psychology
and published some books of children's stories. She also
continued her music studies and composed for the harp.

**NOOR INAYAT KHAN as a baby with her father,
Hazrat Inayat Khan, in Moscow, 1914**

When she was seventeen, Noor fell in love with a fellow music student named
Goldberg. He was a gifted pianist, and he was Jewish. Noor's family objected to their
relationship, even though Goldberg studied to be a Sufi at Fazal Manzil. Their objec-
tion may have been partly because of his religion, but was mainly because he was from a
working-class background, while Noor was descended from royalty. In addition, they felt that
Goldberg was overbearing and needy.

Noor's family was very protective of her, but Noor was stubborn. She and Goldberg got
engaged and stayed together for six years. When World War II began, though, she broke off

Mahākapi Jātaka

Once upon a time when Brahmadatta was reigning in Benares, the Bodhisatta was born of a monkey's womb. When he grew up and attained stature and stoutness he was strong and vigorous, and lived in the Himālaya with a retinue of eighty thousand monkeys. Near the Ganges bank there was a mangotree with branches and forks, having a deep shade and thick leaves, like a mountain top. Its sweet fruits, of divine fragrance and flavour, were as large as waterpots; from one branch the fruits fell on the ground, from one into the Ganges water, from two into the main trunk of the tree.

The Bodhisatta, while eating the fruit with a troop of monkeys thought: "someday danger will come upon us owing to the fruit of this tree falling on the water" and so, not to leave one fruit on the branch which grew over the water, he made them eat or throw down the flowers at their season from the time they were of the size of a chick-pea. But notwithstanding one ripe fruit, unseen by the eighty thousand monkeys, hidden by an ant's nest, fell into the river, and stuck in the net above the king of Benares, who was bathing for amusement with a net above him and another below. When the king had amused himself all day and was going away in the evening, the fishermen, who were drawing the net, saw the fruit, and not knowing what it was, showed it to the king. The king asked, "What is this fruit", "We do not know, sire"

A manuscript page in her handwriting from a story in NOOR INAYAT KHAN'S *Twenty Jataka Tales*

their engagement. She said that she wanted to be free to serve as a nurse on the front lines or get involved in some other way.

MORSE CODE AND SECRET SIGNALS

In 1940, when the Nazis took over France, Noor and her family fled to London. She had also trained as a nurse, so she got a job at a hospital. But it was dull work, mostly chores and no real

NOOR INAYAT KHAN with her brother Hidayat and their mother in Wissous, France, 1921

NOOR INAYAT KHAN (left) with two of her siblings, Khairunissa and Vilayat, in Suresnes, France, 1925

nursing. Noor was anxious to do something more useful to help the Allies. Since her brother Vilayat had joined the Royal Air Force, she decided to volunteer for the **Women's Auxiliary Air Force (WAAF)**.

Noor was assigned to the first WAAF training group for radio operators. First she had physical training, which was difficult because she was petite and uncoordinated. She also had sores on her feet from the constant cold, which made it even harder for her. But she was determined, and she got an A for effort.

She was much better at learning Morse code. She was sent for advanced training and became so fast and efficient that she was picked for a secret signals training course.

RECRUITED BY THE SOE

In 1942, Noor was recruited by the Secret Operations Executive, or SOE. She used the name Nora Baker, to try to hide her Indian heritage and protect her family in case she was ever captured by the Nazis.

The SOE's mission in France was to help the French Resistance sabotage the Nazis, and to prepare them to aid the Allies once they invaded France. The SOE sent weapons, money, and other important supplies, as well as secret agents. In addition, the SOE helped agents and Allied fighters escape from France when it became too dangerous for them to stay.

The SOE was especially interested in Noor because she was bilingual, fluent in French and English. Women had never been sent for wireless operator training, but the SOE wanted Noor. She already knew Morse code, and she was quick.

Wireless operators were the link between SOE headquarters and the agents in France. As a wireless operator, Noor would be responsible for sending messages back to the SOE about arrests, acts of sabotage, and other important news. She would request supplies, and learn when and where supplies and new agents would be parachuted in.

THE WOMEN'S AUXILIARY AIR FORCE (WAAF) was formed in England in 1939, and was linked to the RAF, the Royal Air Force. The WAAF trained women for all military duties except for actually going onto the battlefield. In those days, only men were sent for active duty. If women could take over all the other tasks, then the men would be free to go to battle.

Working as a wireless operator was the most dangerous job in the SOE. When operators were transmitting, the Nazis could easily use **triangulation** to figure out where they were within fifteen or twenty minutes. It was crucial for operators to keep their messages brief. Otherwise, the Gestapo could swoop in and capture them. SOE members didn't wear military uniforms, so they didn't have any protection under international laws of warfare. They were on their own, and if they were caught, would likely be interrogated and shot. Most wireless operators didn't last longer than six weeks before being captured and killed.

TRIANGULATION is a method for pinpointing wireless transmissions. Nazis would cruise the streets holding special radio receivers with revolving antennas to search for radio signals. When they picked up a strong signal, they would tune three separate receivers in different places to that frequency. The intersection of those three places was plotted on a map. Then they would bring a mobile receiver hidden in a van to the area at that intersection, and listen for the signal, which would lead them to the exact location of the wireless transmitter. This method was extremely accurate, and wireless operators had to work quickly before they could be detected. They also tried working at different times, to throw off the Nazis.

Noor would be working with other British officers in France, to help the French Resistance. In addition to her wireless training and teaching her to encode and decode messages, the SOE taught her to use weapons, handle explosives, toss hand grenades, and fight. Even though she was small, she had spunk. She was afraid of firearms, but the SOE gave her a pistol that she was soon prepared to use in self-defense.

She thought a long time about whether she would be able to hurt or kill someone. It was against her Sufi upbringing. But the Nazis had to be stopped. She decided she would do everything she could to fight them. She would shoot or kill the enemy, if she had to.

BLUFF CHECK

The information sent by wireless operators was top secret and had to be trustworthy. But what would happen if Noor was caught? What if she was forced to send false messages, to fool the SOE? How would the SOE know that something was wrong?

The solution for Noor, just as it was for Eddie Chapman, was a bluff check, an operator's unique secret signal to the SOE. In Noor's case, she agreed never to use a phrase containing exactly eighteen letters. If she did, it would be her way of saying that she had been captured and was being forced to send a message by her Nazi captors. As long as there were no phrases of eighteen letters, the SOE would know all was well.

NOOR INAYAT KHAN in London, 1941

FLYING INTO DANGER

On a night in mid-June 1943, under a full moon, Noor was flown to France. She was the first woman to be sent by the SOE to France as a wireless operator. Her code name was Madeleine. The pilot dropped her off in a field in the countryside. All she had with her were her French identity card, her ration book, and her pistol.

Her transmitters and clothing would be flown in later, along with the four boxes of pills given to every agent in case of emergency: one box contained pills that would knock someone out for six hours; one had pills to keep her awake if she was exhausted; one had pills that would cause stomach distress, in case she had to fake an illness; and the last box contained just one pill with a lethal dose of cyanide. If she was captured and facing torture, all she had to do was bite down on the pill, and it would kill her within minutes.

For now, she had to make her way to safety. She didn't know that she was already in more danger than she could ever imagine. The Resistance member who greeted her plane was a traitor, secretly working for the Nazis. He was about to betray her entire network, code name Prosper.

Noor made her way to Paris, and went to the address she had been given. A young man opened the door. For some reason she had been expecting an old lady, but after a few minutes, she took a chance. She used the secret password and he replied with the proper response. She had found her contact.

Without her transmitters, Noor couldn't send a message to SOE headquarters. She was anxious to let them know that she had arrived. Finally she was able to use another agent's equipment. The SOE breathed a sigh of relief. Not only had she arrived safely, but she had contacted them in record time.

CLOSE CALLS

Within days of her arrival, the Gestapo began arresting members of the Prosper network. Noor, at first unaware of these arrests, had her transmitter, but now she had to find a safe place to set it up. This involved unspooling seventy feet of wire for the antenna, without being seen. After transmitting, she would wind it back up and pack everything away. She carried it all around with her in a little suitcase, which was much heavier than it looked. The whole thing weighed over thirty pounds—a lot for a slight young woman to carry.

One evening, Noor was stretching the antenna wire across some trees when suddenly she heard a man's voice asking if he could help her. Noor spun around and was face-to-face with a German officer. Without blinking an eye, she thanked him for his offer. She told him that it would be very helpful. Even though people weren't supposed to have radios, she told him she loved listening to music. If he helped her with the antenna, then she would be able to listen.

Another time, Noor had a close call when she was lugging around her transmitter suitcase. She was stopped by a young German soldier who demanded to know what she was carrying. She told him it was film equipment. He told her to open the suitcase, so she opened it just a bit and said, "Well, you can see what it is. You can see all the little bulbs." The soldier clearly had no idea what she was talking about, but was too embarrassed to say so. He just let her go without looking further.

SENDING MESSAGES ON THE RUN

Noor's first contact was arrested by the Gestapo, along with more Prosper members. And someone had told the Gestapo about Noor and had even given them her description. So she began disguising herself. She dyed her hair red, then blond, then brown again, and she changed her coat, wore hats or scarves, and put on sunglasses. She tried to make herself look Parisian so she wouldn't stand out too much. She was constantly on the move.

All the while, Noor kept writing letters to her family. She never told them where she was or what she was actually doing. They had no idea she was a spy. She didn't want them to worry. The letters were taken by courier to the SOE planes that dropped off supplies, and were flown back to England to be delivered. But the same traitor who had greeted Noor's plane when she arrived in France was making copies of the letters for the Gestapo before sending them on. Now the Gestapo knew all about Noor and her family. They were on the hunt.

Agents were trained never to go to

Type A Mark II suitcase radio, the same kind that was used by **NOOR INAYAT KHAN** in France to send and receive coded messages

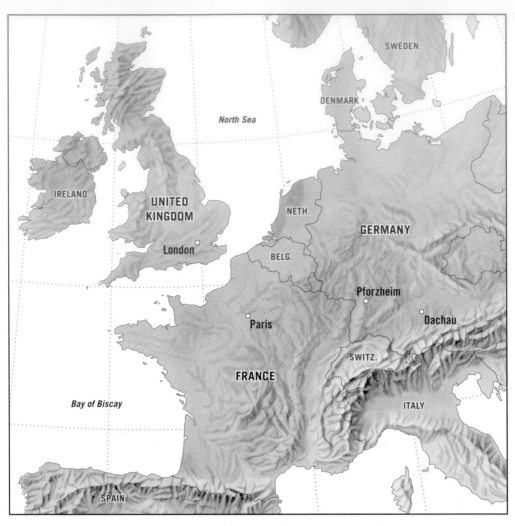

NOOR INAYAT KAHN's work for the SOE began in London, England, and ended behind enemy lines in Dachau, Germany.

places where someone might know them. But Noor panicked and didn't know where else to go. She desperately wanted to continue her crucial work sending messages, but she needed to feel safe. So she returned to the neighborhood where she had grown up, and headed toward her childhood home. Sure enough, a neighbor recognized her. It was just in the nick of time. Her kind neighbor warned her to stay away, that Fazal Manzil had been taken over by the Nazis. Then she invited Noor into her own home to transmit messages. After that, Noor moved on again.

A fellow agent found her a new place to stay. The little apartment was across from Gestapo headquarters on Avenue Foch. She hoped it would be safe. They would never dream of looking for her so close to their headquarters.

Even more members of Prosper disappeared, arrested by the Gestapo, but Noor was still working day and night sending and receiving messages. The SOE eventually demanded that Noor return to London. It was getting much too dangerous for her to stay, and she was valuable. But Noor told them she wouldn't leave. She was the only British wireless operator left in Paris. Finally they convinced her to come back. She was scheduled to fly out in a few days. She would have to wait until the moon was full. That was the only time when there would be enough light for the plane to land.

CAPTURED BY THE GESTAPO

Noor was getting ready to leave Paris. She visited the few contacts she had left to say goodbye. Then she picked up some food and went back to her little apartment. When she walked in, someone was waiting for her. He wasn't an agent. He was from the Gestapo. And he grabbed her.

She fought him with all her strength, scratching, kicking, and even biting him on the hand. He shouted at her but she wouldn't let go. Finally he pushed her off and threatened to shoot her. His hand was bleeding and he was angry. He called for backup. It took several men to get her to their headquarters at 84 Avenue Foch. They took away her transmitter and her codebook, too.

At Gestapo headquarters, Noor was interrogated by an interpreter, but she wouldn't tell him anything. Then she demanded that he let her take a bath. He took her to the bathroom, but left the door open. She yelled at him to treat her with respect and give her privacy. As soon as he had closed the door she locked it, then she slipped through the window and scrambled out onto the roof to get away. When a few minutes had passed, he tried to check on her and realized what she had done. He caught her and brought her back. After that, he kept a closer eye on her.

FUNKSPIEL

The Gestapo had Noor's transmitter, and forced her to send a message to the SOE. They told her what to say. As she tapped out the message, she found a way to include her bluff check—her signal to the SOE to let them know she was in trouble. But the SOE assumed she had simply made a mistake, so they ignored her plea for help.

FUNKSPIEL is a German word meaning "radio game" or "radio play." For the Nazis, it was a counterintelligence operation. When radio operators were taken prisoner by the Nazis, they were forced to send messages to their handlers with false information provided by the Gestapo or Abwehr, in order to trick them. Or else Nazis used their transmitters and sent messages themselves, pretending to be the radio operator.

After that, the Gestapo used her codebook to figure out how to send more messages, all the while pretending to be Noor. They continued this treacherous game, which they called *Funkspiel*—the "radio game"—luring many SOE agents to a terrible fate. As soon as the agents were flown in they would be arrested, and most of them were killed.

ESCAPE

For five weeks, Noor was questioned daily. Her interrogator felt sorry for her and she was treated kindly, but she revealed nothing. She was brave and calm during the day, but at night, when she was alone, she sobbed inconsolably. She couldn't understand how he knew so much about her and her family. Then he showed her copies of some of her letters home. Someone had betrayed her, but she didn't ever find out who it was.

She was confined at night in a locked cell on the fifth floor. There were two other prisoners in the other cells. One of them was a British officer named John Starr. He noticed Noor and decided he would try to make contact with her.

The only time any of the prisoners were left alone was when they were in the bathroom (this one didn't have a large enough window to make an escape). There was a hole in a pipe below the bathroom sink. It would be the perfect place to hide messages. Starr slipped a note under Noor's door when the guard wasn't looking. "Cheer up," it said. "You're not alone. Perhaps we shall find a way to get out of here." Then he told her about the hiding place for messages.

Noor asked her interrogator for pencil and paper. She told him she wanted to write some stories. Then she wrote a reply to Starr and slipped it into the hiding place in the bathroom. Soon they were exchanging messages as often as they could. Starr told her that he and another prisoner were planning an escape. Noor could come with them.

It would to be hard to escape because all the rooms had bars across the windows and skylights. But Starr figured if they had a screwdriver, they could dig into the wooden windowsills around the ends of the bars, in order to remove them. The only problem was, how on earth would they get a screwdriver?

Their chance came when the housekeeper complained that the vacuum cleaner had broken. Starr told her that he could fix it for her. All he needed was some tools. The housekeeper got the okay to bring him the tools, and he fixed the vacuum cleaner, just as he'd said he would. But he fixed it in such a way that it would soon break again. Sure enough, when it failed, she asked him to fix it once more. This time she wasn't paying as much attention to him, and he managed to keep a screwdriver.

Then he hid the screwdriver in the bathroom so that they could take turns digging out the metal bars. It took several weeks. They had to do it when the guards weren't watching. Noor's window was in a skylight, and she had to stand on the edge of her bed to reach it. Starr made a lot of noise whistling loudly to cover up the scraping sounds.

Finally they were all ready. They slipped out during the night and were scrambling across the roof, when a siren began to wail. It was an air raid! The British air force was bombing Paris. The Gestapo always checked on the prisoners during air raids, and would discover that they were missing! Sure enough, as soon as the guards saw the bars on the floor, they knew that Noor, Starr, and the third prisoner, Léon Faye, had escaped up to the roof. The guards went after them, and they were soon imprisoned once more.

NACHT UND NEBEL

Noor was the first British agent to be sent to prison in Germany. It was November 1943. They labeled her "*Nacht und Nebel*"—night and fog. This meant she was destined to disappear into the prison system and never come back out, as though she had disappeared into the night and fog.

She was taken to Pforzheim prison and thrown into a cell. She wasn't allowed to see any other prisoners, and she couldn't ever leave her cell. The guards were warned not to talk to her. They shackled her hands and feet, and then shackled the chains to each other, so she couldn't even sit up straight. They kept her shackled night and day, even when she was eating and sleeping.

It was such inhumane treatment that an elderly prison guard took pity on Noor. Even condemned murderers hadn't been treated so badly. He took off her shackles and let her walk in the prison yard. Although it was forbidden, he spent time talking to her when he could, to keep her spirits up. She told him that she was a British spy, and that she had been captured in France. She told him all about her background and her family, and how much she missed them.

Soon Noor began to practice meditating, as her father had taught her, and she imagined her father singing to her. These were the things that comforted her and helped her to endure her imprisonment—at least during the day.

But every night, Noor's fellow prisoners could hear her sobbing in her cell, and they wanted to comfort her. As Starr did in France, they decided to try to find a way to send her a message, to let her know that she wasn't alone. They scratched a message for her on the bottom of each of their food bowls: "There are three Frenchwomen in cell No. 12." They hoped that eventually she would get one of those bowls and see their message. Soon they got a scratched message back: "You are not alone, you have a friend in cell 1." They continued sending scratched messages back and forth, messages of hope. Noor's last message to them was "I am leaving."

NACHT UND NEBEL, German for "night and fog," was a term the Nazis used to describe how they dealt with prisoners whom they considered most dangerous to their cause. Those prisoners were fated to disappear in Nazi prisons or concentration camps, never to be seen again. In other words, they were murdered.

DACHAU

It was September 11, 1944. Noor had been imprisoned at Pforzheim prison for ten months. The guards took away her clothing that day, and gave her a burlap sack to wear instead. That evening she was sent away, along with three other young women prisoners. Noor recognized one of them from her SOE training.

The four women were taken by train on a long journey. They had no idea where they were going. They were allowed to talk to one another and were given something to eat. It was a small bit of joy during their nightmare existence.

Their destination was **Dachau**, one of the notorious Nazi concentration camps. As soon as they arrived, the other three women were taken out and shot. But the guards threw Noor into a cell. For the next twenty-four hours, she was beaten and tortured. Just before she was shot, her fellow inmates heard her cry out just one word: "*Liberté!*"

"I'M FREE"

For many years after the war, Noor's family and friends had no idea what had happened to her. Even her SOE handler tried to find her without success. It seemed she really had dis-

DACHAU was the first Nazi concentration camp for political prisoners. Over 188,000 people were imprisoned there between 1933 and 1945. From 1940 to 1945, more than 28,000 prisoners died at Dachau, as well as many more who were not officially registered as prisoners (including Noor). Most prisoners who didn't die of disease, starvation, or torture, were shot, hanged, or burned to death in the crematorium.

appeared into the night and fog. Noor's close friend Jean Overton Fuller made it her mission to find out what had happened, and the story of Noor's fate was slowly pieced together.

As Jean searched for clues, she remembered a dream she had had about Noor. It was during the time when the Allies were freeing prisoners from the concentration camps. Jean dreamed that Noor was walking toward her "surrounded by a blue light, her face radiant. 'I'm free,' she said."

Jean told Noor's brother Vilayat about the dream. "He had dreamed the same, he said. I supposed it meant she had been prisoner in a camp which had now been opened, and that she would soon be coming home. He had interpreted it in exactly the opposite sense. 'It means she is dead.'"

Jean tracked down the Gestapo interrogator from Avenue Foch in Paris; Noor's fellow prisoner Starr; some survivors from Pforzheim prison who remembered hearing—and seeing—Noor; the elderly prison guard there who had taken pity on her; and even the cruel Nazi officer

NOOR INAYAT KHAN at age eighteen, 1932

who had beaten and killed her at Dachau. She also discovered that it was the sister of Noor's first contact in France who had betrayed her to the Gestapo.

Eventually, through the testimonies of these many witnesses, Jean learned the story of Noor's fate.

Noor was awarded two posthumous medals to commemorate her courage. England gave her the George Cross, and France gave her the Croix de Guerre with Gold Star. Today, in London, there is a statue commemorating the brave Sufi Princess Spy who lost her life in the fight against the Nazis.

The Nazis weren't the only enemy of the Allies during World War II. The Japanese army was in league with the Nazis, fighting in another part of the world. And Roy Hawthorne, a Navajo code talker, was one of the brave people who helped defeat them.

SEVEN

Roy Hawthorne
NAVAJO CODE TALKER HERO

A SECRET MESSAGE

Khac-da.

Bih-tsee-dih bi-yah al-tah je-jay.

Ah-da-ah-ho-dzah.

A secret coded message like this was transmitted over the airwaves in the South Pacific sometime in 1942. The Axis enemy, listening in, was stymied. What language was this? It didn't sound like English, yet it was coming from American Marines. It definitely wasn't the listener's native language, Japanese.

Japan's code breakers worked night and day on the mysterious transmission. They were certain they would be able to figure it out; after all, they'd broken every other code used by the Americans. But this one was different.

Then came the reply:

Be-zonz aganh-tol-jay bilh-higih ye-el-tsanh

What were the Americans saying?

In fact, there were only twenty-nine people in the whole world who could understand this message. They were a special group of US Marines. And they were Navajo.

> **Khac-da (Ambush)**
>
> **Bih-tsee-dih bi-yah al-tah-je-jay (Base under attack)**
>
> **Ah-da-ah-ho-dzah (Desperate)**
>
> **Be-zonz aganh-tol-jay bilh-bigih ye-el-tsanh (Aerial relief within sight)**

GROWING UP NAVAJO

The Navajo, or Diné, are a Native American people who live mostly in the Southwestern US. Roy Hawthorne was born on the

Navajo code talker **ROY HAWTHORNE** in uniform

Navajo reservation in 1926, and was raised according to traditional Navajo customs. He said his background, "as was with all Navajo [children], was to take care of the family's herds of sheep. . . . In my day, growing up in the Navajo Nation . . . people didn't have jobs, had very little funds. Food was scarce, as was everything else. . . . It's no longer like that, but we had sheep, we had horses and cattle. And so our job was to take care of the livestock. That was the lifeblood of the Navajo family."

The Navajo had always herded sheep, as far back as anyone could remember, and traveled with their flocks and lived off the land. Then, in 1864, the US government banished the nation to a barren place three hundred miles away from their homeland. This forced migration, called the Long Walk, was a terrible time in Navajo history. Many Navajos perished along the way. Women who stopped to give birth during the journey were mercilessly killed, along with their infants. Anyone who tried to help them was killed, too.

The Navajos' new home didn't have enough land for their livestock. There was no clean water, and nearly one-third of the people there grew sick and died. Finally, four years later, a treaty was signed. The treaty allowed the Navajos to return to a reservation on their homeland, where, in the decades following, they once again prospered.

Then, during the Great Depression of the 1930s, when Roy was a child, a law was passed calling for the destruction of most of the Navajo livestock. Government officials came to the reservation. They threw sheep and goats into pits where they were burned alive. Cows and horses were shot. The government claimed this mass slaughter had to be carried out because there was too much livestock in too small an area, and the land was being overgrazed.

In fact, the US government was trying to erase the Navajo culture. Navajo people were still considered second-class citizens. They didn't have the same rights as other Americans. They weren't allowed to vote and they were not treated with respect. Many white people called them savages. In addition to the government taking the Navajos' livelihood away, it also took Navajo children from their families. Children like Roy were sent to federal schools, where they were forced to speak only English and to give up their Navajo traditions. Anytime the students spoke in Navajo, they were punished.

Pretty quickly, these Navajo children became fluent in English. But despite the government's efforts, many of them who still had access to their families continued to speak Navajo at home, as well as when they were alone with their friends and schoolmates.

WAR WITH JAPAN

The emperor of Japan wanted to take over Asia and the Pacific, starting with an invasion of Manchuria in 1931. His army invaded China in 1937. In 1940, Japan joined forces with Nazi Germany and Italy as part of the Axis alliance. After Japan bombed **Pearl Harbor** in Hawaii, in December 1941, US President Franklin Roosevelt declared war on Japan.

On December 7, 1941, Japanese fighter planes bombed the US naval base at PEARL HARBOR, near Honolulu, Hawaii. The next day, US President Franklin D. Roosevelt declared war on Japan. Three days after that, Germany and Italy joined Japan to declare war on the US.

The Marines came to the Navajo reservation to recruit in 1942. Joining the Marines was a way for young Navajo men to escape poverty. They had heard about the Japanese bombing of Pearl Harbor. They felt that an attack on the US was an attack on the Navajo Nation as well. Roy Hawthorne explained, "We loved the land where we lived, and it was embedded in our genes that no enemy from across the water or anywhere would take it from us." Despite the way the US government had treated them, they would wear their uniforms with pride.

Before they left the reservation, most Navajos took part in a special ceremony called the **Blessingway Ceremony**. This rite was performed to protect them before going into battle, and many of the Navajo soldiers who had shipped out would continue to perform this ceremony every morning until they had returned home.

The young Navajo men who enlisted were sent to boot camp, like all the other Marine recruits.

A Navajo BLESSINGWAY CEREMONY is for protection, to restore balance and avert misfortune. It might be used to protect the home, or a pregnant woman, or a child going through puberty. In Roy Hawthorne's case, it was intended to protect a man who was going off to war. The ceremony usually lasts two nights and features a singer chanting special songs over the person being blessed. At the end of the ceremony, there would be a blessing of the person's body, using corn pollen, and they would be given some pinches of corn pollen to eat. After that, the person would be given the bag of pollen to use for themselves. Many Navajo soldiers would perform a Blessingway Ceremony each morning while at war.

Boot camp was grueling. The recruits were drilled and trained in the basics: using weapons, working together as a group, and following orders without question. They also had to get used to shouting. In the Navajo culture people didn't yell at each other, so for some recruits it was a hard adjustment when their commanding officers barked orders at them.

But the Navajo recruits had been raised to be tough. They were already used to waking up early to tend the sheep. They were used to hard work. They were strong and they learned quickly. Roy felt that "when the time came to serve our country in the military, the transition wasn't as difficult as it was for other ethnic groups."

But once they had completed basic training, they discovered that the service the Marines had in mind for them was a different kind of work entirely.

AN UNBREAKABLE CODE

The Japanese army was brilliant at breaking codes. Japanese code breakers would sometimes even interrupt coded transmissions to taunt their enemy, saying that

ROY HAWTHORNE with his young bride, Jayne, at Fort Campbell, Kentucky

they couldn't wait to hear the Allies' next message. Throughout World War II, they were able to break every code they came across—except one.

Navajo is an oral language—spoken, but not written. In fact, there was no written alphabet for Navajo until recently. (In the mid-1900s, some non-Navajos came up with a way of writing the language down. Now there is even a Navajo font for use on computers, but the language is still primarily an oral one.) Those who know Navajo don't ask "Do you *speak* Navajo?" Instead, they ask "Do you *hear* Navajo?" Navajo children learn the language by listening.

The sound of Navajo is very different from most other Native American languages. It includes rising and falling tones, and glottal stops (sounds made by stopping the air as it passes through your throat).

Philip Johnston was four years old in 1896, when his father was sent as a missionary to the Navajo reservation. Even though he wasn't Navajo, Philip learned to speak Navajo pretty well, although he never mastered the language completely.

Philip served in the army during World War I. When World War II began, he had the brilliant idea to use Navajo as a code. Navajo Marines could work in pairs: one would send a message and the other would receive it. Nobody except another Navajo would be able to understand. Philip was confident that the Japanese didn't have any Navajo speakers in their army. It would be perfect!

His idea wasn't entirely new. During World War I other Native Americans, including people from the Choctaw and Comanche nations, worked as code talkers, sending messages in their respective languages. But after the war, Germany sent people to the US to learn those languages. There was a good chance that the enemy might understand them, if they were used as a code again in World War II.

The Navajo, however, were an isolated nation. Very few non-Navajos spent time with them. Their language was not related to any other Native American language. And it was such a difficult language that nobody would be able to speak or understand it anyway, unless they had grown up speaking Navajo.

WOULD IT WORK?

Philip had to convince the Marines that using Navajos to send coded messages was a good idea. The Marines devised a test. Two Navajos were put in separate rooms. Then they had to send messages to each other by field telephone.

"Begin withdrawal at 2000 today."

"Enemy expected to make tank and dive bombing attack at dawn."

"Two officer prisoners en route to your headquarters."

Each message was dictated to the first Navajo in English. He translated in his head as he listened, and immediately spoke the message into the phone in Navajo. The second Navajo was listening, and immediately translated in his head and wrote down the message in English. The whole process took just a few minutes.

Normally, coded messages could take several hours to send; they had to be carefully translated into Morse code and sent by radio, *dit-dah-dah*. Then the message had to be decoded and written down. It was easy to make mistakes, and the whole process took time.

By contrast, the Navajo Marines were able to send messages in just a minute or two. After many tests, with no mistakes, their superior officers were convinced.

THE FIRST CODE TALKERS

A group of thirty Navajo Marines were taken to a building, away from the other recruits, and locked in. Their mission: come up with a code—in Navajo—to be used in war.

Now, instead of being punished for speaking Navajo, as many of them had been in school, these men were being *ordered* to speak Navajo!

They would have to learn their code by heart. And, most important, they were warned not to talk to anyone else about it. Ever. Not their families, not their friends, not other Marines. They couldn't even talk about it with one another outside of that building. It was top secret.

The group worked hard to develop their code. The notes they kept during these sessions were locked up at night. They couldn't take them out of the classroom, to study. In spite of the restrictions, Roy said, "It wasn't difficult. It was a matter of working at it day and night to memorize. We had to memorize the entire code, because it was not permitted to have anything written—no books or anything like that." The men's Navajo upbringing served them well: with no written language, they had always relied on their memories. Now they used that skill to make up a code and memorize it.

First, they started with a basic alphabet code. They picked English words that started with each letter of the alphabet, then translated the words into Navajo.

For instance, for the letter "a" they picked the word "ant." In Navajo, the word for ant is *wol-la-chee*.

For "r" the word was "rabbit," which is *gah* in Navajo.

For "m" the word was "mouse," which is *na-as-tso-si* in Navajo.

For "y" the word was "yucca," which is *tsah-as-zih* in Navajo.

So to spell out the word "army" in Navajo code, they would say *wol-la-chee gah na-as-tso-si tsah-as-zih*.

After a while, they realized that it would take too long to spell out every single word. There were some words that would surely be used often. They could simply translate them directly into Navajo. For instance, the word "attack" was *al-tah-je-jay* in Navajo. "Retreat" was *ji-din-nes-chanh*.

There were also many words that didn't have Navajo translations. For instance, there were no words in Navajo for modern military terms, for the names of other countries, or for the months of the year. They would have to find Navajo words to represent them. These had to be words that would be easy to remember. After much discussion, they came up with Navajo words for them all.

For instance, "submarine" was *besh-lo*, which is Navajo for "iron fish."

"Battleship" was *lo-tso*, which is Navajo for "whale."

"December" was called *kesh-mesh*, the Navajo word for "Christmas."

And the word for "America" was *ne-he-mah*, which means "our mother."

Messages sent in Navajo code could only be understood by a Navajo code talker. Even another Navajo wouldn't understand, unless he had been trained as a code talker. Any other Navajo hearing these messages would hear a string of unconnected Navajo words that didn't make any sense.

Roy remembered a wartime story from a Navajo friend who wasn't a code talker. "One morning, he heard Navajo language coming over his radio, and what he heard were words like 'potatoes' . . . and 'eggs.' . . . So he said, 'These guys are down there having a picnic!' But actually . . . they were sending a message about bombs and hand grenades. A 'bomb' in Navajo code would be an 'egg' and a 'hand grenade' in Navajo code would be a 'potato.'"

TESTING THE CODE AND TRICKING THE COAST GUARD

Once the code had been developed and memorized, it had to be field-tested. The code talkers performed the test in California. Roy recalled, "It was highly classified. Nobody knew anything about the program. When it was field-tested, the Coast Guard on the West Coast . . . [picked up] the signal. They became very nervous because they thought the language was Japanese, and that the Japanese had overrun positions in California. I like to point out that it was just simply a group of Navajo teenagers who confused the Coast Guard of California! That code was ready to be deployed on the battlefield, which it [soon] was. And there it was found to be effective, and continued to be effective all during the war."

Roy noted that at the time the code was implemented, "the Japanese were actually winning the war. The outlook for victory for America was dismal, because when the Americans were planning an attack on the Japanese, who held certain islands, the Japanese would have already discovered this by breaking the code that existed at that time. So they knew exactly where it was going to happen. They would thank the Americans, and say, 'We'll be there.' And they were.

Bougainville, Solomon Islands, December 1943: Two Navajo code talkers serving with a Marine signal unit operate a portable radio set in a clearing they've hacked in the dense jungle behind enemy lines.

Ballarat, Australia, Army Air Force base, July 7, 1943: These Navajo code talkers are cousins, attached to a Marine artillery regiment in the South Pacific. They'll relay orders over a field radio using the Navajo code.

When the code talkers arrived, the whole scene of battle changed and the Americans began winning the war."

After the code had been field-tested, it was time to send Navajo code talkers into battle. Twenty-nine of the thirty original code talkers went to the Pacific. (The other man ended up joining the army and was sent to Germany, where he was killed in action.)

In 1943, an additional two hundred Navajo code talkers were trained and sent to the Pacific. That was when Roy joined up, at the age of seventeen. That group was followed by another two hundred. With each new group they added new words to the Navajo code, which all had to be memorized, too.

In all, more than four hundred Navajo code talkers served in World War II. Of those men, thirteen were killed in action.

FIGHTING AND SENDING MESSAGES IN THE PACIFIC WAR

Code talkers generally worked in pairs, sending and receiving messages from another pair of code talkers. One would send the message while the other would crank the radio transmitter to give it power. They would take turns doing each task. They had to work quickly and then speed away. Even though the enemy couldn't understand what they were saying, they could still figure

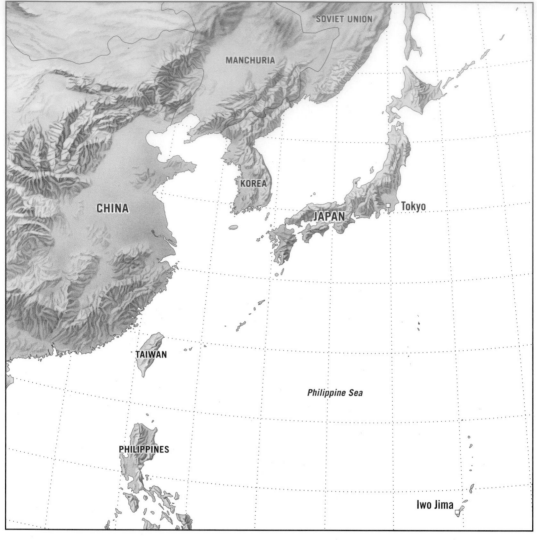

The portion of the Pacific Theater where **ROY HAWTHORNE** and other Navajo Code Talkers were posted during the war.

out where they were transmitting from and would try to kill them—if they could catch them.

All the men in Roy's family served in the military, and some of them were also code talkers. At one point during the war, he experienced quite a coincidence. "There was a Navajo way, a Navajo custom," Roy explained, "that you would always ask, 'Where are you from?' and 'What clan are you from?' So I asked the person on the radio these questions. And he told me his name, and it turned out he was one of my cousins and that he was not very many miles away. He was in a different [Marine] division. So we got together and visited. . . . At home, he lived only a hundred miles away from my home, but that was too far to travel. . . . Travel was difficult in those days, in the '40s, particularly on the Navajo reservation. There were no roads, no telephones. . . . So the war brought about things of that nature."

In addition to sending messages, Navajo code talkers "took part in every Marine battle in the Pacific War. Each of the six Marine divisions had code talkers."

Roy was with the First Marine Division. He recalled that "code talkers were many times assigned to combat patrol or observation patrol. And we'd go out and either seek out the enemy and make an attack, or simply observe." While on patrol one day, the antenna of Roy's radio was shot off and he couldn't use it. "We came over the top of a ridge, and at that point, the enemy . . . opened fire on our patrol while we were pinned down, and there was no way to counter that. . . . The Japanese were numerically superior to us at that time.

"So, my radio was out of commission and we couldn't call for reinforcements or make a report, or do anything with the radio. So I said to the patrol commander, 'I can run down there where the machine guns are all placed, I can run down there and I can knock those guns out.' He said, 'No, your job is to man that radio. So go ahead and get that thing back in action.' Fortunately, I [figured out how to fix it] . . . and I was able to call for an air strike, which came right away and helped us. . . . There were many situations similar to that.

"During an attack, you don't have any time to be afraid. You're concentrating on destroying the enemy. And although it's almost imminent that the enemy will destroy you, you're not thinking about that. You're thinking about destroying the enemy. So fear comes later."

TAKING BACK IWO JIMA AND HELPING TO WIN THE WAR

While other Marines could take leave from battle from time to time, the Navajo code talkers had to stay. Their work was simply too important. They were needed every second.

Without the code talkers, the US would not have been able to retake the island of Iwo Jima. This island was a particularly important place for the Allies. Because of its location, off the southern coast of Japan, it was the perfect place for Allied fighter planes to stop and refuel. If the

Allies couldn't land there, it would prove nearly impossible to make an aerial attack on Japan.

On March 16, 1945, after a weeks-long and bloody battle, a Navajo code talker transmitted the following message:

Than-zie tlo-chin: Ashdla Chal Din-neh-ih.

Bi-tsan-dehn: Hash-kay-gi-na-tah taa n-kih tsostsid Tabaha.

Ah-di a-la-ih tseebii nos-bas-nos-bas Shi-da Klesh ma-e ah-jad be-la-sana ah-tad gah tse-nill tkin dibeh ah-jah be a-kha tsah lin-daa tsaa a-la-ih hastaa ashdla. Tkin gloe-ih a-kha yil-doi a-chi be-tas-tni tse-nill ye-dshe-al-tsisi-gi. Ba-ha-this.

To: VAC (5th Amphibious Corps)

From: CO 327th Regiment

At 1800 US flag raised on Hill 165. Iwo Jima secure. Over.

KEEPING A SECRET FOR TWENTY-SIX YEARS

When the war ended, the code talkers were told they could never speak about what they had done—not even among family. Roy noted, "I had two brothers and several cousins who served as code talkers, and we never spoke of it, never told our parents about it. . . . We were instructed when we were discharged that we would keep it secret. And that's what we did, for twenty-six years."

Navajo code talkers returned from the war to life on the reservation, without a hero's welcome. They came back to lives of poverty, where they were still being treated as second-class citizens. They still didn't have the right to vote.

Once they were home, many Navajos participated in the **Enemy Way Ceremony**. This was a traditional Navajo healing ceremony, to help warriors returning from battle. The ceremony

An **ENEMY WAY CEREMONY** is a special Navajo healing ceremony for a soldier who has been in combat or has been imprisoned or wounded. It can help to banish the ghosts and trauma of war—what many might also call post-traumatic stress—so that the soldier can regain balance with the universe. (The Navajo term for this balance is *Hozho*.) The soldier's family will find a spiritual leader or medicine man to talk to the soldier about his experiences at war, in order to determine what kind of ceremony would work best. The ceremony includes prayers or songs, and family members often participate.

would get rid of the ghosts of anyone a warrior might have killed. It would also banish nightmares and depression after the horrors of war.

Twenty-six years later, Roy remembered, "The government came out and said, 'It's okay for you to talk about it now.' And we joked about it and said, 'We thank the government for giving us twenty-six years to prepare some good war stories!'"

ROY HAWTHORNE being honored by President George H. W. Bush. Later, in 2001, Roy received the Congressional Silver Medal from President George W. Bush. An inscription on the back of the medal is written in Navajo and translates to "With the Navajo language they defeated the enemy."

HONORING THE NAVAJO CODE TALKERS

In 2000, the bravery and ingenuity of the Navajo code talkers was finally acknowledged when the Honoring the Code Talkers Act was signed into law. At a ceremony at the White House in July 2001, President George W. Bush presented Congressional Gold Medals to the original twenty-nine Navajo code talkers. Of the twenty-nine, only five were still alive, and only four were able to attend the ceremony in person to receive their medals. Roy was honored when Congressional Silver Medals were given to the rest of the Navajo code talkers later that year.

After the war, Roy converted to Christianity and became a minister. He also served as president and vice president of the Navajo Code Talkers Association, and volunteered extensively in the Navajo Nation, in Arizona, where he helped to build schools where students are encouraged to speak both English and Navajo.

Roy died on April 21, 2018, at the age of ninety-two.

Roy Hawthorne used his specialized language skills to help confuse and combat the enemy. World War II spy Moe Berg also used his language skills to fight the Axis powers—when he wasn't playing major-league baseball.

EIGHT

Moe Berg
MAJOR-LEAGUE SPY

PLAYING THE GAME

"**Can any of** you fellows catch?" Ray Schalk was the reserve catcher and manager of the Chicago White Sox, but he had a broken thumb. Both backup catchers were also out with injuries. Schalk was desperate to find someone on his team to fill in.

Twenty-five-year-old Moe Berg had been playing with the team for a year, since 1926. He told Schalk he *used* to think he could catch. Schalk asked Moe who had told him he couldn't, and Moe said it was his high school coach. Schalk told Moe to prove his coach wrong. And boy, did he ever!

Moe's hitting was not the best, but as it turned out, according to baseball historian Ralph Berger, Moe "was an excellent defensive catcher. Possessing a strong arm, he could gun down the swiftest base runners." With his knowledge of baseball strategy and his study of the hitters, he could call the games with great skill. Suddenly Moe was in demand.

He played baseball with major-league teams for fifteen years. But he also played another, far more dangerous game. Moe Berg was a spy.

GROWING UP

Morris "Moe" Berg, born in New York in 1902, was the youngest of three children of Jewish immigrants from Ukraine. His father was a hardworking pharmacist who moved his family to a middle-class neighborhood in New Jersey when Moe was eight years old. He wanted his family to have all the advantages they hadn't had in Eastern Europe.

There were two things Moe liked more than anything else: learning new things and playing baseball. When he was just a toddler, he wanted to go to school like his older brother and sister. He eventually ended up at Princeton University, as one of the very few Jews there, and he threw himself into his education.

But when Moe wasn't studying, he spent every spare moment playing baseball. He was on the Princeton team and known as "the brainiest man in baseball." Moe and his second-base teammate would sometimes talk strategy with each other in Latin, so the opposing team wouldn't understand them. Moe paid for his education by playing ball all summer long. His father didn't understand his son's love of baseball. During Moe's entire career, his father never attended a single one of his games.

MOE BERG in his Princeton University baseball team uniform

A SHOW-OFF AND A LONER

Moe was fascinated by languages and he studied as many as he could. In addition to Latin, he dabbled in Greek, French, Hebrew, Spanish, Italian, German, Sanskrit, Japanese, Chinese, Korean, Arabic, Hindi, Portuguese, and Hungarian. He never actually claimed to be fluent in any of them, but he liked to give people the impression that he was.

He also liked to read as many newspapers as possible. He developed a lifelong habit that had him up every morning and heading out to buy a pile of them from the newsstand, including foreign ones. He would sit with a cup of coffee and read, read, read. Sometimes he cut out articles to keep.

It would take a while for him to finish all the newspapers, and he left them out all over his room. If anyone tried to move them or clean them up, Moe would get angry. He said that the unfinished newspapers were still "alive," and he forbade anyone to touch them until he was done.

When he was playing baseball, he would bring newspapers or books with him to the dug-out and read until it was his turn to bat. He was often seen reading scholarly books or doing a crossword puzzle.

Moe was a bit of a show-off, and perhaps reading all those academic books and newspapers was his way of demonstrating how smart he was. He didn't ever have to say it; everyone else would assume as much when they saw him engrossed in his reading.

Moe was also a loner, and he had some other odd habits. He liked to take baths several times a day. Even when he was staying at someone's house, he would disappear to bathe.

He also dressed in the same clothes every day: a black suit with a white dress shirt, a black tie, black shoes, and a gray hat. For most of his life, Moe never varied this outfit. He would wash out his garments at night, hang them up to dry, and then put them back on the next morning.

For all his quirks, Moe could also be very charming. He would very happily talk for hours with friends and acquaintances before disappearing for whatever reason. Nobody knew where he went or what he did.

TO PARIS AND BACK AGAIN

Moe graduated from Princeton in 1923. That June, he signed with his first major-league team, the **Brooklyn Robins**.

At the end of baseball season, in October 1923, Moe moved to Paris to continue his studies. He enrolled at the Sorbonne, where he took twenty-two courses, learning about everything from Medieval Latin to French linguistics to Italian literature. He wandered the city, practiced his French, and read piles and piles of newspapers.

He returned to the US in time for spring training, after which he played on several smaller teams for a while. Then

THE BROOKLYN ROBINS were originally called the Brooklyn Dodgers. In 1914 the name was changed to honor the team's manager, Wilbert Robinson. When Robinson retired in 1931, the team went back its original name.

Moe decided he wanted to go to law school. He enrolled in Columbia University to study law in 1924—before leaving partway through his courses to take up baseball again.

Moe's pattern continued for several years. In 1926, he joined the Chicago White Sox. He played for a while and then took some time off to continue his law studies. Then he took a leave of absence from school in order to play baseball. Finally, in 1930, he graduated with a law degree, and in 1931 he got a job at a law firm in New York, where he worked for a few years—except during baseball season, when he continued to play for the White Sox.

A SPY IN THE MAKING

Early in Moe's baseball career, he seemed to be a gifted all-around player. Then when he was recruited for the major leagues, his limitations began to show. He was a slow runner, an inconsistent pitcher, and a lousy hitter. According to Ira Berkow, a sportswriter who got to know Moe and wrote a lot about him, "He was a marginal player, but he had a fifteen-year career . . . and he was a linguist and he majored in languages. And the saying was that he knew ten languages, but he couldn't hit in any of them."

MOE BERG in September 1933, catcher for the Washington Senators

However, he was a great catcher.

There was another reason the major leagues wanted Moe. There were a lot of Jews living in New York, and a good way to bring them to the ballpark was to advertise that there was a Jewish player on the team. At the time, there weren't many Jews playing pro baseball. Although Moe wasn't religious, he didn't mind at all that being Jewish had helped him land a spot with the Brooklyn Robins.

In 1932, Moe joined the Washington Senators. Then he was invited to go to Japan with two other ballplayers to coach Japanese baseball teams. He loved Japan and learned Japanese fairly quickly. He wasn't completely fluent, but he learned enough to get around. When his colleagues returned to the US, Moe stayed abroad until early 1933, touring Asia, India, and the Middle East.

Back in the US, he continued to play for the Senators, then left that team and joined the Cleveland Indians. But when he was invited back to Japan in 1934 as an interpreter for an All-Star team with Babe Ruth, Lou Gehrig, and other greats, he was delighted to return there to talk baseball. However, he also had another item on his agenda, a secret plan that he told no one.

He brought with him a brand-new movie camera. One day during his stay in Tokyo, he put on a kimono and disguised himself as a Japanese man. He hid the camera under his kimono and went to a hospital in one of the tallest buildings in the city. He had a bunch of flowers and said in Japanese that he was visiting a patient. Once he got in, he dumped the flowers and snuck up to the top floor, where he filmed footage of the city of Tokyo. He included the shipyards, factories, railway yards, and military installations. When he was done, he smuggled the camera back out under his kimono.

The Japanese were very strict about allowing foreigners access to the city of Tokyo. Foreigners weren't allowed to photograph military installations, harbors, or other **landmarks**, but Moe,

For governments that keep an eye on one another, even during peacetime, it's obvious why foreign military installations would be important LANDMARKS to monitor. But shipyards, rail yards, and factories can also provide crucial information. During World War II, an increase in train frequency could indicate preparation for battle. At that time, most supplies were sent by train. If ships appeared heavier, by sitting lower in the water, that might mean that they were filled with equipment or supplies, and if they looked higher in the water, that would mean they weren't carrying a heavy cargo. If they arrived at port looking heavy and left lighter, it would mean they had just delivered a shipment, and vice versa. An increase in production at a factory might be a tip-off that battle preparations were being made. For instance, a factory that manufactured weapons or military vehicles would need to increase production before an invasion. The type of photo surveillance Moe carried out could provide this kind of important information to officials who knew how to analyze it.

for all his affection for Japan, didn't care about such rules. He far preferred to live by his own. In accessing a forbidden view of the city, Moe had successfully carried out a secret mission of his own making. He decided that he would make a very good spy.

A GREAT STORYTELLER

Moe loved telling stories. All the US sportswriters liked to interview him because of that. They called him "the most famous linguist in baseball." No matter what they asked him about, he could talk endlessly and keep everybody interested. One sportswriter referred to him as "the Professor."

"Moe was really something in the bullpen," agreed a former teammate. "We'd all sit around and listen to him discuss the Greeks, the Romans, the Japanese, anything. Hell, we didn't know what he was talking about, but it sure sounded good."

He once told a journalist a story about meeting Albert Einstein when he was at Princeton. He said that he went to Einstein's house, and Einstein said to him, "If you teach me baseball, I will teach you the theory of relativity." According to Moe, Einstein then thought better of that idea, saying, "We better forget about that, because you would learn the theory of relativity faster than I would learn baseball."

When the US joined World War II, Moe decided it was finally time to tell someone the story of his trip to the hospital roof in Tokyo.

MAN OF MYSTERY

In 1942, Moe wrote to the OSS. Now that the US was at war with Japan he was sure they would be very interested in seeing the forbidden footage he had taken of Tokyo. He later even claimed that his film helped the US to plan bombing raids over Tokyo. However, this is doubtful, as the film was already eight years old by the time the US was bombing the region, and therefore wouldn't have provided entirely accurate information.

Of course, that didn't stop Moe from boasting about it.

Moe applied to work as a spy for the OSS, and in 1944 his application was accepted. His excellent skills as a catcher provided good spy train-ing. "Baseball is all about espionage," said George F. Will, the *Washington Post* columnist who's known as much for his political coverage as for his love of baseball. "Catchers are being spied on all the time—that's why they hide their signals to the pitcher down in their crotch."

"Baseball is a game of deception, secrets, and strategy . . . [and] Moe's role as catcher was, in a way, the head deceiver, so the skills he learned as a baseball player served him well as a spy," according to film director Ben Lewin, who directed the 2018 film about Moe's life, *The Catcher Was a Spy.*

Moe went through basic spy training and waited for his first assignment. Meanwhile, when he wasn't playing ball, if any of his baseball acquaintances saw him he would pretend not to know them. If they tried to talk to him, he would warn them away by putting his finger to his lips and shushing them. He was very good at creating a mysterious aura, though his strange tactics were not ones most spies would use to truly **blend in**.

Unlike Moe Berg, most spies work hard to avoid drawing attention to themselves. They're usually very careful to BLEND IN with their surroundings and learn local customs so that they won't stand out. For instance, US agents stationed in Europe during WWII would be cautioned to hold cigarettes in the European way, between their pointer finger and thumb, rather than the American way, between index finger and pointer finger. When Sufi Princess Spy Noor Inayat Khan went to France, one of her colleagues noticed that when she served tea, she poured the milk into her cup before pouring in the tea. This was the British way of pouring tea. (In France, they would pour in the tea first and then add milk.) Noor was reminded to pour her tea the way locals would, or else someone might figure out that she wasn't really French.

BOMBS AND GUNS

During World War II, a crucial question loomed in the Allies' minds: How close were the Nazis to developing a nuclear bomb? American physicists were working on the bomb's development, but everyone knew that the Germans had brilliant scientists. If Germany developed a bomb first, it could help Hitler win the war.

For his first mission, Moe was sent to Europe to meet with physicists who had fled Nazi

Germany, and try to help determine how far along the Germans' research was. He flew to London by military transport for his briefing. During the flight, his newness to the spy trade was on full display when his pistol fell out of his pocket and into the lap of his fellow passenger, Major George Shine. Moe apologized, saying that he wasn't used to carrying a gun. He put it back in his pocket and it fell out again. Finally, Major Shine offered to stow it for him in his bag until they landed.

After a brief stay in London, Moe flew to Algeria, and from there to Italy, where he met with the physicists and learned as much as he could. Some months later, he returned to London to await his next orders.

ORDERS TO KILL

Werner Heisenberg was a famous German physicist who was working for the Nazis. His area of expertise was nuclear physics. If anyone was working on a nuclear bomb, it would be Heisenberg. The question was this: Was he working on a nuclear bomb, and if so, how far had he gotten on it? A trusted colleague had assured Berg that while Heisenberg was a loyal German, he was most definitely anti-Nazi. But the OSS had to be certain that Heisenberg posed no threat.

The OSS learned that Heisenberg was going to be giving a lecture in Zurich, Switzerland, that December. Moe's mission was to go to the lecture and decide just how close Heisenberg was to developing the bomb, and then take necessary steps.

According to a colleague, Moe told him that "he'd been drilled in physics, he'd had a lot of one-on-one training, and had been told to listen for certain things. If anything Heisenberg said convinced him the Germans were close to a bomb, then his job was to shoot him—right there in the auditorium. It probably would have cost Berg his life—there would have been no escape." He had a cyanide pill hidden in his pocket, just in case he'd have to take his own life before he could be captured.

That December, Moe went to Zurich for the lecture, under cover as a Swiss graduate student. Nobody there recognized him as a famous baseball player.

He patted his pocket to make sure the gun was securely in place. Then he sat back in his chair.

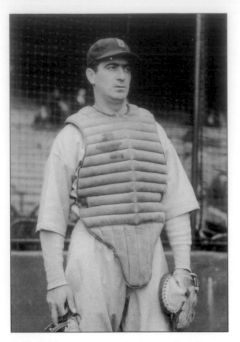

MOE BERG, catcher for the Boston Red Sox

The lecture hall was full. Moe scanned the audience and took notes: "Nazi," he wrote, describing one man seated near him; "sinister eyes," he wrote about another.

Heisenberg began his lecture. Moe listened, trying to make sense of what Heisenberg was saying. His German wasn't completely fluent, but he had been briefed on what to listen for and he was a quick study. He also concentrated on the reactions of others in the audience. He would know if Heisenberg said anything of interest.

In fact, Heisenberg made no mention of nuclear bombs or the science that would allow their development. He spoke about something else entirely. Moe's career as a brilliant catcher had prepared him well for spy work, and in this instance, he determined that there was no danger. Robert Rodat, a screenwriter for *The Catcher Was a Spy*, noted that as a great catcher, Moe could sense "when a runner was going to steal, and even though Heisenberg was trying to hide it, Berg knew he was despondent because Germany didn't have the bomb and was going to lose the war."

The pistol stayed in his pocket and the cyanide pill went unused. Both Heisenberg and Moe walked away from the lecture. Mission accomplished.

SHHHHH!

For the rest of his life, Moe continued to be secretive. Even when he no longer worked as a spy, he acted as though he still was. If anyone asked him about what he was doing, he'd shush them.

He was awarded the **Medal of Freedom** after the war, but refused to accept it because he couldn't tell anyone about what he had done to earn it. The Medal of Freedom is America's highest honor to civilians whose actions have aided in the war effort of the US and its allies.

Moe stopped playing baseball after fifteen years in the major leagues. In the end, he had played for the Brooklyn Robins/Dodgers, the Chicago White Sox, the Boston Red Sox, the

Baseball cards depicting MOE BERG, coach of the Boston Red Sox in 1940

Cleveland Indians, and the Washington Senators. From time to time, he still stopped by the ballpark and chatted with the journalists and the other players.

He continued his habit of voraciously reading anything he could get his hands on, and he still disappeared mysteriously from time to time.

Eventually Moe moved in with his brother, and lived with him for many years. When his brother died, Moe moved in with his sister. He never married and never had children.

Shortly before his death in May 1972, Moe said, "Maybe I'm not in the Cooperstown Baseball Hall of Fame like so many of my baseball buddies, but I'm happy I had the chance to play pro ball and am especially proud of my contributions to my country. Perhaps I could not hit like Babe Ruth, but I spoke more languages than he did."

The last thing he did before he died was to ask his nurse, "How did the Mets do today?"

THE MEDAL OF FREEDOM is a decoration established by President Harry S. Truman to honor civilians whose actions aided in the war efforts of the US and its allies. This esteemed honor was also presented to Nancy Wake—code name White Mouse—an Australian woman who worked with the SOE. She parachuted into France in 1944 to coordinate Resistance activities there, working with the Maquis.

After Moe died, his sister accepted his Medal of Freedom on his behalf. The medal is part of the collection at the Baseball Hall of Fame. Moe Berg baseball cards are now considered to be collector's items, and some of them are on display at CIA headquarters.

NINE

There were many more surprising spies who took part in World War II. Some spied for the Allies, some for the Axis powers, and some were double and triple agents who spied for both!

Here is a brief introduction to several of these surprising spies whose efforts, for better or worse, made history.

VELVALEE DICKINSON: THE DOLL LADY

One of the oddest tales of a World War II enemy spy in the US is the story featuring Velvalee Dickinson, known as "the Doll Lady." She and her husband moved from California to New York City in 1937, and opened a doll shop on Madison Avenue. Collectors from all over the world bought and sold antique dolls from the Dickinsons' shop. But it turned out that Velvalee was dealing in more than just dolls.

Some time after the shop opened, several of Velvalee's customers started receiving letters in their mailboxes that were marked "returned to sender." The letters had all been mailed to the same address in Buenos Aires, Argentina. But the customers who received them hadn't mailed any letters to Argentina! Who had sent them to Buenos Aires, and why? And why were the letters finding their way back to Velvalee's customers' mailboxes?

The letters themselves were notes concerning repairs to various dolls. One letter, supposedly from one of Velvalee's customers who lived in Oregon, mentioned "three Old English dolls" that had been sent for repairs to a doll hospital.

Another letter, supposedly from a customer in Ohio, mentioned a "Mr. Shaw, who had been

VELVALEE DICKINSON'S notorious doll shop in New York Cityk

ill but would be back to work soon." This Ohio customer, of course, had no idea who Mr. Shaw was, and had not written the letter.

These customers, and others, contacted the FBI and showed them the mysterious letters. After a lot of sleuthing, the FBI figured out that the letters were coded messages meant for the Japanese Army.

The "three Old English dolls" referred to three warships that had been sent to a shipyard—not a doll hospital—for repairs.

"Mr. Shaw" referred to the USS *Shaw*, a US warship that had been damaged during the attack on Pearl Harbor. It was being repaired and would soon be back in service.

The FBI determined that Velvalee had been recruited by the Japanese when she lived in California. They were paying her lots of money to get information and send them coded messages about the condition of the US Navy's ships, especially ones that had been damaged at Pearl Harbor.

Her instructions were to mail the messages to an address in Buenos Aires, where they would

Mug shots from the FBI file of **VELVALEE DICKINSON**, "the Doll Lady"

be picked up by a Japanese spy. However, something must have happened to the spy, because he wasn't picking up the letters. That's why they got sent back to the US—returned to sender.

To make the letters seem authentic, Velvalee had used the names and addresses of real people: her doll shop customers. She had even forged some of their signatures. Of course, she never expected that they would actually see those letters.

In 1944, Velvalee was convicted of espionage and was told by the court, "The indictment to which you have pleaded guilty is a serious matter. It borders on treason." She was sentenced "to the maximum penalty provided by the law, which is ten years and $10,000 fine." In fact, she was released from prison in 1951 after having served only seven years. She returned to New York and worked in a hospital. She died in obscurity in 1961.

KIM PHILBY AND THE CAMBRIDGE FIVE SPY RING

Kim Philby was one of the most talented spies in history. He worked for the British secret service, and over the years advanced to positions of great authority within MI5.

But Kim Philby had a secret.

Kim Philby was a double agent.

When Kim was younger, he'd attended Cambridge University in England. While he was a student, he was approached by the Soviet secret service to spy for them, and Kim agreed.

From then on, the entire time he worked at MI5, both during and after World War II, Kim was secretly passing British intelligence to the Soviets. He got away with it until 1963, when he was discovered and nearly captured before he fled to the USSR, where he lived for the rest of his life.

Kim Philby was part of what became known as the Cambridge Five spy ring: five British students at Cambridge University who were recruited as Soviet spies in the 1920s and 1930s. The other four were Anthony Blunt, Donald Maclean, Guy Burgess, and John Cairncross. They all went on to work for the British government while betraying it.

The Cambridge Five were open to being recruited because they were drawn to the idea of Communism. In a Communist society, there is no privately owned property. Everything is owned and controlled by the government. The Soviet Union was a Communist nation; England was not.

At that time, England didn't consider the Soviet Union to be an enemy. However, in August 1939 the Soviets signed a non-aggression pact with Hitler that changed everything.

In 1939 England was at war with Hitler. The non-aggression pact between Germany and the Soviet Union meant England and the Soviets were now enemies—and the Cambridge Five's treasonous activities were even more serious than they had been when England and the Soviet Union had been on friendlier terms.

The secret non-aggression pact lasted for two years, until Hitler violated it by attacking Soviet troops in eastern Poland. Now the Soviets were fighting Germany—and that meant they were England's ally again.

All of these complications trickled down to the Cambridge Five. The alliance between England and the Soviet Union meant that the Cambridge Five were still betraying England by leaking secrets to the Soviets—but they were also helping their Soviet comrades to battle the Nazis.

When World War II ended in 1945, the Cold War era began. The Cold War was a conflict between the US and the former Soviet Union. Instead of violence, the two countries used verbal, ideological, and economic weapons against each other. Because England was an ally of the US, that alliance meant England and the Soviet Union were once again enemies. All the information the Cambridge Five had previously passed along to the Soviets could still be used against

England. And each of the Cambridge Five continued to spy for the Soviets after World War II, doing more damage to England with their betrayals.

John Cairncross was stationed at Bletchley Park in 1941, and the Soviets later awarded him the Order of the Red Banner for his help in providing information about the German military. This was one of the highest Soviet military awards, given for extraordinary heroism, dedication, and courage. Then in 1944 he was posted to MI6, where he worked in counterintelligence under none other than Kim Philby. He claimed he didn't know that Kim or the other Cambridge Five members were fellow Soviet spies.

In 1951, when both Donald Maclean and Guy Burgess were in danger of having their covers blown, Anthony Blunt helped arrange their successful escape to Moscow. By that time John Cairncross was also suspected of being a spy, but there wasn't enough evidence to prove it. At that point he stopped spying for the Soviets. He left England for the United States, and taught at Northwestern University in Chicago. He later moved back to Europe and lived in Italy, then in France. In 1979 a British journalist unearthed the truth about John, who made a full confession but received no punishment. In 1997 John Cairncross published his memoir, *The Enigma Spy*, in which he described his life and work as a Soviet spy.

Meanwhile, after the war, Anthony Blunt became a leading British art historian. He was knighted and served as an art advisor to Queen Elizabeth until 1964, when an American agent he had tried to recruit as a Soviet spy at Cambridge back in 1937 betrayed him to British Intelligence. In exchange for immunity, he made a full confession to MI5. They agreed to keep his secret for fifteen years. In 1979, after a journalist discovered what Anthony had done, British Prime Minister Margaret Thatcher publicly revealed his secret, and his knighthood was taken away. He was dismissed from his various art historian roles. He died of a heart attack in 1983.

IAN FLEMING: 007

Before he wrote novels about Agent 007, James Bond, author Ian Fleming worked for British Naval Intelligence. According to William Stephenson, chief of British Intelligence during World War II, "Fleming was always fascinated by gadgets." James Bond's exploits were inspired by Fleming's experiences in the secret service. Since they were fiction, his James Bond books weren't prohibited by the Official Secrets Act. Fleming helped come up with the idea for Operation Mincemeat (page 115) and invented the backstory for the make-believe Major William Martin.

IAN FLEMING at his desk at Mitre Court, 1961

ROALD DAHL: ON A SECRET MISSION

Best known as the author of beloved children's books including *Charlie and the Chocolate Factory*, Roald Dahl was also a pilot for the British Royal Air Force during World War II. After he was injured in a crash, he took on a role working for the British secret service. He was posted to the British embassy in Washington, D.C., so that he could make friends with socialites and important people who had political connections. His mission was to get them on his side, so that they would help convince the US government to join England in the fight against the Nazis.

While he was in the US, he was also recruited by an MI6 covert espionage network stationed in New York. The network's goal aligned with Roald's original mission, to encourage the US to join England in the war. To do this, the network planted anti-Nazi and pro-British articles in US newspapers. After the US entered the war, their goal was to encourage the US to continue to fight. Roald's mission was to spy on the US and let MI6 know if he heard anything of interest from the high-level politicians and diplomats he met through his new socialite friends.

While Allied and Axis spies were at work during World War II, there were also hundreds of unexpected heroes whose courageous efforts helped the Allied cause in countless ways. Here you will meet just a few of them. They include a witch, a chef, a mime, a corpse, a champion cyclist, and some intrepid teenagers.

DOREEN VALIENTE: CODE BREAKER AND WITCH

Doreen Valiente was a linguist working as a shorthand typist when she was recruited to work at Bletchley Park. There she most probably translated decoded German messages into English. Later she was moved to London to work with Bletchley Park's Government Code and Cipher School. Because of the Official Secrets Act, she was never able to reveal exactly what she did at Bletchley Park.

But Doreen became known for another reason: she was a well-respected witch. Doreen said she had her first vision, or magical experience, when she was a child. She practiced spells throughout her young life, and then in 1953 she was initiated as a Wiccan. She eventually became a high priestess, and is considered by the English Wiccan community to be the "Mother of Modern Witchcraft."

English Wiccan **DOREEN VALIENTE**, seen here with some of the tools of her trade. She also worked at Bletchley Park during World War II.

JULIA CHILD: COOKING UP A DISGUSTING RECIPE

Many years before world-famous chef Julia Child learned how to cook, she worked for the OSS. In fact, according to the CIA, during the time she worked for the OSS "Julia was self-admittedly a disaster in the kitchen. Perhaps all the more fitting that she soon found herself helping to develop a recipe that even a shark would refuse to eat." Shark attacks were a common problem for the military, which had large-scale operations going on at sea during World War II.

This photo of **JULIA CHILD** was taken by Paul Child in Ceylon (now Sri Lanka) in 1944, when she was working for the OSS.

In addition, curious sharks had a tendency to bump up against torpedoes, exploding them before they reached their target. So the OSS put together a committee to invent a shark repellent. Julia helped to come up with the recipe, which apparently smelled like a dead shark. It was successfully used by the military until 1970, and may even have been used by NASA to keep sharks away from returning space equipment that had landed in the ocean.

MARCEL MARCEAU: SILENT SCOUT

The famous French mime Marcel Marceau was also a member of the Resistance during World War II. He made false IDs for Jews to hide their religious identity. He also saved the lives of many Jewish children by leading them to safety in Switzerland, all the while disguised as a troop guide with his "Scouts." He used his talent for mime to entertain the children during the difficult journey.

GINO BARTALI: CYCLING HERO

Gino Bartali was a champion cyclist in Italy who had won the Tour de France in 1938. During World War II, at the request of the Archbishop of Florence, he joined a secret network to help to protect Jews and others in Italy who were at risk from the Nazis and Mussolini. The network was looking for someone to transport false papers from the hidden printing press that made them to the people who needed them. So Gino was their courier. He rolled up the papers and hid them inside the handlebars and frame of his bike. Then he smuggled them right under the noses of Mussolini's men, who happily cheered their beloved cycling champion as he rode past on his long training rides.

OPERATION MINCEMEAT: THE CORPSE THAT FOOLED THE NAZIS

The body of British Major William Martin was found floating in the water off the coast of Spain. The Spanish fisherman who discovered it could tell that it had been in the water for a while. At least, it looked that way.

It was assumed that Major Martin had been on a downed aircraft. Chained to his wrist was

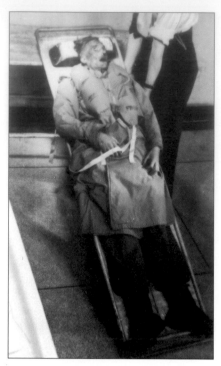

This body on a stretcher, later identified as **GLYNDWR MICHAEL**, was used in Operation Mincemeat as part of an odd but successful World War II deception.

a briefcase that contained a letter marked "Personal and Most Secret." It described plans for an invasion of Greece by Allied forces.

The fisherman alerted Spanish authorities to the body. At that time, Spain was not officially involved in the war, and Spanish authorities wanted their country to remain neutral. They gave a copy of Major Martin's Personal and Most Secret letter to Germany's Abwehr before returning it to the British. The plans outlined in the letter convinced the Nazis to shift their troops in preparation for an Allied invasion in Greece.

In fact, it was all a trick. There was no Major Martin. The body was that of a Welshman named Glyndwr Michael, who had died after accidentally eating rat poison. His parents were no longer living and there were no other relatives to claim his body, so after consultation with forensic experts, British Intelligence decided he could serve as the fictional Major Martin. Major Martin's body, along with the letter containing false information, would be placed off the coast of Spain in the perfect spot for Spanish fishermen to find it.

The deception—known as Operation Mincemeat—was the idea of intelligence officer Ian Fleming, and it was carried out by agents Ewen Montagu and Charles Cholmondely. They wrote the "secret" letter with the expectation that Spain would pass it along to the Germans, and they created a persona for the corpse in order to make the trick more credible.

Operation Mincemeat indeed fooled the Nazis into expecting an invasion in the wrong place. As Nazi troops gathered in Greece, waiting for the Allies to arrive, the real invasion was successfully carried out in Sicily.

Glyndwr Michael was eventually laid to rest in Spain near the place where his body had been found. On his headstone is the name William Martin. His real name, Glyndwr Michael, was added later, when the British government revealed his identity. There's also a plaque on a war memorial in his birthplace in Wales, commemorating him as "The Man Who Never Was."

YOUNG HEROES AND SUBVERSIVE ACTS

Many brave teenagers—and even children—helped the Resistance in France and elsewhere during World War II.

In Le Chambon-sur-Lignon, France, Pierre Piton worked with the Resistance when he was eighteen years old. Disguised as a Scout leader, he guided small groups of Jewish refugees on a perilous journey to safety in Switzerland. After making twenty such trips, he was arrested by an Italian border patrol and handed over to the French gendarmes, many of whom were unwillingly under the Nazis' control and who often subverted the Nazis by secretly helping refugees or warning them of danger. The gendarmes released Pierre after three months in prison, telling him that they knew what he was doing. They congratulated him for his noble work—but they warned him not to do it anymore.

Paul Majola, a shepherd boy also from Le Chambon-sur-Lignon, was just nine years old when he began helping the Resistance. He picked up forged papers from a farm where Resistance counterfeiters worked. The forgers hid the papers for Paul in an empty beehive and in the grave of the farmer's mother, where the police would never think of searching. Paul would then distribute the papers to other Resistance fighters and refugees in the region.

Peter Feigl was a Jewish refugee from Austria who was living in France during World War II. He worked with the Resistance when he was fourteen years old, helping to spy on German soldiers and translate documents. He also sabotaged Nazi trucks by pouring sugar into the gas

PAUL MAJOLA, age nine, in
Le Chambon-sur-Lignon, France

PETER FEIGL (smiling, bottom row, fourth from left) with his fellow "Boy Scouts," setting off to help the Resistance in France during their school holidays

This is a twenty-franc French banknote with a Hitler head attached, as described by PETER FEIGL. He and his friends helped the Resistance by making and distributing these banknotes in France. It was a subtle and clever revolt against Hitler and the Nazis.

tanks and puncturing the tires, and he went along on a mission to blow up a factory that had been commandeered to manufacture equipment for the Nazis.

When he was fifteen, Peter and a small group of other Jewish refugees, disguised as Boy Scouts, spent their winter break from school helping the Resistance. One of their most subversive acts was to distribute anti-Hitler material. They found discarded envelopes from mail sent from Germany, and removed the Hitler stamps. Then they cut Hitler's face from the stamps and glued the faces onto French twenty-franc notes. These notes had an image of a fisherman hauling his net from the sea. Peter and his friends attached the Hitler face just above the rope in the fisherman's hands, making it look like the fisherman was choking Hitler. These altered banknotes carried their anti-Hitler message wherever they were spent.

TEN

TOOLS OF THE TRADE:
SECRET MESSAGES AND CODES

INVISIBLE INK

Spies often have to write messages or notes in a way that keeps them hidden from the enemy. Juan Pujol Garcia, for instance, used invisible ink to write secret messages between sentences he had written in regular ink. Invisible ink was also used to write important military information on Josephine Baker's sheet music.

Invisible ink can be made from different substances, some of which you can find in your very own home. All you need is juice from half a lemon (or you can use orange juice, milk, or equal parts baking soda and water mixed together) and a cotton swab (or other writing implement such as a paintbrush, feather, toothpick, stick, or even the tip of your finger).

To create the ink:

- Squeeze the lemon juice into a bowl.
- Dip the cotton swab (or other writing instrument) in the
  lemon juice and use it to write your message on a piece of paper.
- Let it dry.

To reveal the message, you'll need a heat source. (Check with an adult before using a heat source.) You can use a non-halogen light bulb or an iron. Hold the paper above the light bulb. The heat from the bulb will make the message appear. If you use an iron, set the paper on an ironing board. Use a high setting and move the iron back and forth quickly across the paper until the message is revealed. Don't hold the iron down on the paper for too long or the paper might burn.

Another way to reveal your message is to paint over the paper with dark juice, such as cranberry, raspberry, or purple grape.

Here are two more methods for writing an invisible message:

- Write your message on white paper using a white crayon. To make the message appear, paint over the paper with some watercolor paint. The wax in the crayon will repel the paint and the message will appear. You can also use dark juice instead of watercolor paint.

- Take two sheets of white paper. Place one on top of the other. Write your message using a pen or pencil. Make sure to press down hard as you write. Then discard the top piece of paper. The second piece of paper will have indentations on it from your writing. To make the message appear, shade over the paper with the side of a pencil point. The message will appear in the indentations beneath the shading.

CIPHERS AND CODES

Many spies use ciphers and codes to communicate, but what's the difference between the two? Actually, they're similar, and there's a lot of overlap, so it can be confusing. Here's a basic description of each.

Ciphers

A cipher is a way of hiding the meaning of a sentence by using a different symbol for each letter of the alphabet. When a spy translates a message into a cipher, she is *enciphering* the message. When another spy who has received that message figures out its meaning, he is *deciphering* the message.

Morse code actually works like a cipher because each letter is represented by another symbol.

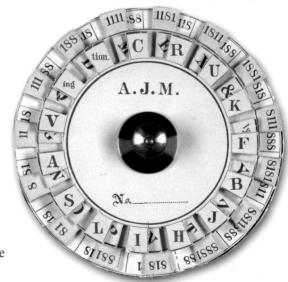

A CIPHER DISK provides an easy way to encipher letters, by simply turning the disks to align the letters with numbers on the outer circle. This cipher wheel (or disk) is from the American Civil War.

Codes

A code is a way of hiding the meaning of a sentence, phrase, or word by using a different, agreed-upon sentence, phrase, or word in its place. When a spy translates a message into code, she is *encoding* the message. When another spy who has received that message figures out its meaning, she is *decoding* the message.

Eddie Chapman used his laughing sign as a code in his radio transmissions. He and his handler decided ahead of time that each variation of his laughing sign would have a different meaning. "Hu hu hu" would mean that he had no new information. "Hi ha hu" would mean he was going to Berlin. "He he he" would mean he was going to America. Nobody else knew about this secret code, so they wouldn't know what it meant.

Pig Latin is a common code. To encode a sentence into Pig Latin, take the first letter of each word and move it to the end of that word, followed by "ay." For vowels, insert the letter "w" before the "ay." So, "Here is the secret message" would be "Ere-hay is-way e-thay ecret-say essage-may."

NAVAJO CODE

Navajo code talkers like Roy Hawthorne used both a cipher and a code to communicate. They started with an alphabet cipher, where each letter of the English alphabet was represented by a Navajo word. Later, they added a code, using specific Navajo words to represent words in English.

Here is the alphabet cipher part of the Navajo code, revised in June 1945. The English translation of each Navajo word is in parentheses. You will note that in some cases there's more than one option for each letter. That's because after the code was first devised, the code talkers decided to add more words for some of the letters to make it more difficult for the Axis powers to crack the code. The additions also made it more difficult for the code talkers, as they had to memorize all those extra words.

Navajo Code

A WOL-LA-CHEE (ant)
BE-LA-SANA (apple)
TSE-NILL (axe)

B NA-HASH-CHID (badger)
SHUSH (bear)
TOISH-JEH (barrel)

C MOASI (cat)
TLA-GIN (coal)
BA-GOSHI (cow)

D BE (deer)
CHINDI (devil)
LHA-CHA-EH (dog)

E AH-JAH (ear)
DZEH (elk)
AH-NAH (eye)

F CHUO (fir)
TSA-E-DONIN-EE (fly)
MA-E (fox)

G AH-TAD (girl)
KLIZZIE (goat)
JEHA (gum)

H TSE-GAH (hair)
CHA (hat)
LIN (horse)

I TKIN (ice)
YEH-HES (itch)
A-CHI (intestine)

J TKELE-CHO-GI (jackass)
AH-YA-TSINNE (jaw)
YIL-DOI (jerk)

K JAD-HO-LONI (kettle)
BA-AH-NE-DI-TININ (key)
KLIZZIE-YAZZIE (kid)

L DIBEH-YAZZIE (lamb)
AH-JAD (leg)
NASH-DOIE-TSO (lion)

M TSIN-TLITI (match)
BE-TAS-TNI (mirror)
NA-AS-TSO-SI (mouse)

N TSAH (needle)
A-CHIN (nose)

O A-KHA (oil)
TLO-CHIN (onion)
NE-AHS-JAH (owl)

P CLA-GI-AIH (pant)
BI-SO-DIH (pig)
NE-ZHONI (pretty)

Q CA-YEILTH (quiver)

R GAH (rabbit)
DA-NES-TSA (ram)
AH-LOSZ (rice)

S DIBEH (sheep)
KLESH (snake)

T D-AH (tea)
A-WOH (tooth)
THAN-ZIE (turkey)

U SHI-DA (uncle)
NO-DA-IH (Ute)

V A-KEH-DI-GLINI (victor)

W GLOE-IH (weasel)

X AL-NA-AS-DZOH (cross)

Y TSAH-AS-ZIH (yucca)

Z BESH-DO-TLIZ (zinc)

Can you decode this message?
(See page 146 for the answer.)

KLIZZIE NE-AHS-JAH TLO-CHIN BE

GLOE-IH TLO-CHIN GAH KLIZZIE-YAZZIE !

TSAH TSE-NILL A-KEH-DI-GLINI BE-LA-SANA YIL-DOI A-KHA

MOASI TLO-CHIN LHA-CHA-EH AH-NAH TKIN DIBEH

LHA-CHA-EH TKIN MA-E CHUO YEH-HES TLA-GIN

NO-DA-IH NASH-DOIE-TSO D-AH .

TSAH-AS-ZIH NE-AHS-JAH SHI-DA

WOL-LA-CHEE AH-LOSZ DZEH BE-LA-SANA

KLESH SHI-DA BI-SO-DIH DZEH AH-LOSZ

DIBEH BI-SO-DIH TSAH-AS-ZIH !

MORSE CODE

Many spies, including Noor Inayat Khan and Virginia Hall, used Morse code to send secret messages. Morse code is alphabetic, which means there's one symbol for each letter of the alphabet. It's made up of dots and dashes, which are arranged in a different way for each letter. In Morse code, a dot is called "dit" and a dash is called "dah." If you say those words out loud, "dit" sounds short and "dah" sounds long. And that's the way it sounds when a message is sent.

During World War II, wireless operators used a special machine with a lever to send Morse code messages. They tapped on the lever quickly for "dit" and held it down longer for "dah." Whoever received the message would hear electronic beeps that would sound short for "dit" and long for "dah."

There are many instances of spies sending Morse code messages in other ways, too—including with their own bodies. For instance, a prisoner might tap on the wall in Morse code to communicate with the prisoner in the next cell. A quick tap would be a "dit" and a tap with a pause would be a "dah."

In a Somali prison in 1981, Mohamed Barud was serving a life sentence, being held in solitary confinement, for the crime of writing a letter of complaint about conditions at a local hospital. Dr. Adan Abokor, a doctor from that hospital, was being held in the next cell. Abokor managed to get a message to Barud that he would "talk" to him through the wall by tapping in code. He began by tapping out the alphabet, so that Barud could figure out the code he was using. They communicated that way for two years. Then the doctor got his hands on a copy of *Anna Karenina*, a Russian novel by Leo Tolstoy. He tapped the entire story in code to Barud as a way of helping to keep him distracted from his despair. In 1989, a few years after the start of the Somalian Revolution, Barud and Abokor were both released from prison.

One of the most famous examples of physically communicating Morse code is US Navy Commander Jeremiah Denton's brave tale. On July 18, 1965, when he was on a flying mission during the Vietnam War, he was shot down and taken prisoner by the North Vietnamese army. He spent most of the next seven years and seven months in solitary confinement. Ten months after his capture, he was forced by his captors to speak in a propaganda film, where they ordered him to say good things about his treatment. But as he spoke, he was able to blink a Morse code message: T-O-R-T-U-R-E. This was the first confirmation that the North Vietnamese were torturing US prisoners of war. Denton was released in 1973.

Some spies found ways of sending Morse code messages by knitting the code into clothing. Just as Morse code has two different symbols, dot and dash, knitting is done with two different stitches, knit and purl. Stitches could be knit or purled to create a Morse code message, but the person knitting them wouldn't look suspicious. Phyllis Latour Doyle worked for the British secret service and took advantage of that fact. She parachuted into occupied France in 1944 and knit Morse code messages about everything she found out while spying on the Germans there.

Another way knitters used their craft to record information was to keep track of passing trains by dropping a stitch (which leaves a hole in the knitting) every time a train would pass. This method of counting could be used for collecting other, similar types of information without drawing attention.

The most famous Morse code message is:

· · · — — — · · ·

It looks like the letters SOS, without spaces between the letters. It's used as a call for help. Some people think it stands for "Save Our Ship" or "Save Our Souls," but it doesn't actually stand for anything. It's just a simple code that's easy to remember.

If you learn the Morse code alphabet, you can send secret messages yourself by tapping out the letters. Remember to insert a longer pause after each letter. You can also try other ways of using Morse code, by saying "dit" and "dah" out loud for the letters, or by blinking a message.

For practice, see if you can figure out the message on page 127. There are no separations between the sentences, so you'll have to figure that out, too. (The answer is on page 146.)

MORSE CODE

Alphabet

A .—
B —...
C —.—.
D —..
E .
F ..—.
G ——.
H ....
I ..
J .———
K —.—
L .—..
M ——
N —.
O ———
P .——.
Q ——.—
R .—.
S ...

T —
U ..—
V ...—
W .——
X —..—
Y —.——
Z ——..

Numbers

0 —————
1 .————
2 ..———
3 ...——
4 ....—
5 .....
6 —....
7 ——...
8 ———..
9 ————.

Can you decode this message?

(See page 146 for the answer.)

···· ‒ · ‒ · ‒ ‒ ‒ ‒ ‒ ‒ · · ‒ ‒ · ‒ · · · ‒ ‒ · ‒ · · ‒ ‒ · ·

‒ · · · · · · · ‒ ‒ ‒ · · · · · ‒ ‒ ‒ · · ‒ · · · · ‒ ·

‒ · ‒ ‒ ‒ ‒ ‒ · · ‒ · ‒ ‒ · · · ‒ ‒ · · ‒ · ‒ ‒ ‒ ·

‒ · ‒ ‒ ‒ ‒ · · ‒ · ‒ · ‒ · · ‒ ‒ · · ‒ · · · ‒ · ·

‒ ‒ ‒ · ‒ · ‒ ‒ ‒ ‒ ‒ · · ‒ · ‒ · ‒ ‒ ‒ · ‒ ‒ · ‒ ‒

‒ ‒ ‒ ‒ · · · · · ‒ · ‒ ‒ · ‒ ‒ ‒ · ‒ ‒ ‒ ‒ ‒ · ·

··· ‒ ‒ · ‒ · ‒ ‒ !

TIME LINE

1923 Moe Berg signs with his first major-league team, the Brooklyn Robins.

1923 Moe Berg studies in Paris.

1924 Moe Berg enrolls in law school at Columbia University.

1925 Josephine Baker moves to Paris and opens in *La Revue Nègre*.

1926 Josephine Baker is the most financially successful black woman in the world.

1926 Moe Berg joins the Chicago White Sox.

1927 Moe Berg is discovered to be a great catcher.

1930 Moe Berg graduates from law school.

1932 Moe Berg joins the Washington Senators.

1932 Moe Berg goes to Japan as a baseball coach.

JANUARY 30, 1933 Adolf Hitler becomes chancellor of Germany.

1934 Eddie Chapman pulls off first big robbery with the Jelly Gang.

1933–34 Moe Berg joins the Cleveland Indians.

1934 Moe Berg returns to Japan and makes a secret film of Tokyo.

AUGUST 2, 1934 Hitler proclaims himself *führer*—he is now the dictator of Germany.

1937 Josephine Baker marries Jean Lion and converts to Judaism.

MARCH 12, 1938 Germany takes over Austria.

1939 MI9 is established.

1939 Eddie Chapman is arrested in England and jumps bail.

MARCH 11, 1939 Eddie Chapman is caught and sent to jail in Jersey.

MARCH 15, 1939 German troops occupy Czechoslovakia.

MAY 22, 1939 Italy joins forces with Germany (but doesn't join the war until June 10, 1940).

AUGUST 1939 Soviets and Germans sign secret non-aggression pact.

SEPTEMBER 1, 1939 Germany invades Poland.

SEPTEMBER 3, 1939 Britain and France declare war on Germany—World War II begins.

1940 Josephine Baker is recruited as an honorable correspondent and begins to spy for the French Resistance.

1940 Jasper Maskelyne signs up for the British army and is sent to the Western Desert in North Africa.

JANUARY 23, 1940 Code breakers at Bletchley Park crack Enigma code.

MAY 15, 1940 The Netherlands surrenders to Germany.

MAY 20, 1940 Nazis open Auschwitz, a concentration camp in Poland.

MAY 28, 1940 Belgium surrenders to Germany.

JUNE 10, 1940 Italy joins the war as an Axis nation.

JUNE 22, 1940 France surrenders to Germany.

JULY 16, 1940 The SOE is founded in England, to "set Europe ablaze" (Winston Churchill).

SEPTEMBER 13, 1940 Italy invades Egypt.

SEPTEMBER 27, 1940 Japan joins Germany and Italy in the Axis alliance.

1941 Josephine Baker goes to North Africa and becomes gravely ill.

1941 Juan Pujol Garcia offers to spy for the Nazis.

1941 Jasper Maskelyne supposedly makes Suez Canal disappear and hides Port of Alexandria.

1941 Virginia Hall is recruited by the SOE.

JUNE 22, 1941 Germany invades the Soviet Union.

AUGUST 23, 1941 Virginia Hall arrives in France under cover as a journalist.

OCTOBER 1941 Eddie Chapman is released from jail in Jersey.

DECEMBER 1941 Eddie Chapman is arrested and sent to prison in France.

DECEMBER 7, 1941 Japan bombs Pearl Harbor.

DECEMBER 8, 1941 US and Great Britain declare war on Japan.

DECEMBER 11, 1941 Hitler declares war on the US.

1942 First group of Navajo Marines begin training as code talkers.

1942 Jasper Maskelyne tricks Rommel in North Africa.

1942 Noor Inayat Khan joins the SOE.

1942 Moe Berg tells the OSS about his film of Tokyo.

1942 Virginia Hall is on the Gestapo's most-wanted list.

APRIL 1942 Juan Pujol Garcia is brought to London by MI6.

APRIL 10, 1942 Eddie Chapman joins the Abwehr.

JUNE 1942 Eddie Chapman's first mission: parachute into England.

JUNE 13, 1942 The OSS is founded in the US.

NOVEMBER 1942 Virginia Hall flees France on foot.

DECEMBER 1942 Eddie Chapman joins MI5.

1943 Roy Hawthorne joins the US Marines.

FEBRUARY 1943 Eddie Chapman "blows up" the de Havilland factory in England, with help from Jasper Maskelyne.

MARCH 1943 Eddie Chapman is awarded the Iron Cross, Germany's highest honor, while betraying the Nazis right under their noses.

MAY 13, 1943 German and Italian troops surrender in North Africa.

JUNE 16, 1943 Noor Inayat Khan is flown to France.

AUGUST 1943 Moe Berg joins the OSS.

OCTOBER 13, 1943 Noor Inayat Khan is arrested by the Gestapo.

SEPTEMBER 8, 1943 Italy surrenders to the Allies.

NOVEMBER 26, 1943 Noor Inayat Khan is sent to Pforzheim prison in Germany.

1944 Moe Berg joins the OSS and goes on his first mission.

1944 Juan Pujol Garcia helps the Allies pull off the Normandy invasion by tricking the Germans into thinking the invasion would happen elsewhere.

1944 Eddie Chapman parachutes into England a second time.

1944 Virginia Hall joins the OSS and returns to France, where she makes contact with the Maquis and arranges parachute drops.

June 6, 1944 D-Day—Allied forces begin invasion of occupied France.

JULY 29, 1944 Juan Pujol Garcia is awarded the Iron Cross, Germany's highest honor, while tricking them into thinking he was loyal to them.

SEPTEMBER 12, 1944 Noor Inayat Khan is transported to Dachau and murdered.

NOVEMBER 1944 Eddie Chapman is dismissed from MI5.

1944 Eddie Chapman finds his girlfriend, Betty Farmer.

DECEMBER 1944 Juan Pujol Garcia receives MBE (Member of the Order of the British Empire) award in a private ceremony.

DECEMBER 1944 Moe Berg attends Heisenberg's lecture with a gun.

FEBRUARY 23, 1945   American flag is raised on Mount Suribachi on the strategically important island of Iwo Jima in the Pacific Theater. By the end of March, after heavy losses, US troops complete their takeover of the island, thanks in part to the work of the Navajo code talkers.

MAY 1945   Virginia Hall becomes the only civilian woman in World War II to receive the Distinguished Service Cross, awarded in a private ceremony by US President Harry Truman.

APRIL 28, 1945   Benito Mussolini is captured and hanged by Italian partisans.

APRIL 30, 1945   Hitler commits suicide.

MAY 7, 1945   Germany surrenders to the Allies—the war is over in Europe.

MAY 8, 1945   V-E Day (Victory in Europe)

AUGUST 15, 1945   Japan agrees to surrender to the Allies.

SEPTEMBER 2, 1945   Japanese sign surrender agreement; V-J Day (Victory over Japan).

OCTOBER 1945   Moe Berg is given the Medal of Freedom, but he turns it down.

1946   Josephine Baker is awarded La Médaille de la Résistance avec le grade d'officier for her work helping the French Resistance.

JANUARY 1946   Moe Berg resigns from the OSS.

JANUARY 16, 1946   Noor Inayat Khan is posthumously awarded the Croix de Guerre with Gold Star (the highest civilian honor in France).

1947   Josephine Baker marries Jo Bouillon and they adopt their "Rainbow Tribe" of children.

1948   Virginia Hall joins the CIA.

APRIL 5, 1949   Noor Inayat Khan is posthumously awarded the George Cross (the highest civilian honor in Britain).

SEPTEMBER 29, 1952   Jean Overton Fuller's book is published, detailing the life and ultimate fate of her friend Noor Inayat Khan (republished with additional details in 1988).

1954   The first version of Eddie Chapman's memoir is published: *The Eddie Chapman Story*, by Frank Owen.

1959   Juan Pujol Garcia vanishes.

1961   Josephine Baker is named a Chevalier de la Légion d'Honneur.

1966   The revised version of Eddie Chapman's memoir is published: *The Real Eddie Chapman Story*.

JULY 9–10, 1971   Navajo Code Talkers Association is formed at a reunion of sixty-nine code talkers. In addition to honoring the code talkers, the association's objectives include educating Navajos as well as the general public about their important role during World War II.

May 29, 1972   Moe Berg dies after asking his nurse, "How did the Mets do today?"

MARCH 1973   Jasper Maskelyne dies in Kenya.

April 14, 1975   Josephine Baker dies in Paris just days after opening in a grand show about her life. She is the first American woman to merit the honor of a twenty-one-gun military salute at her funeral.

JULY 8, 1982   Virginia Hall dies in Maryland.

AUGUST 14, 1982   President Ronald Reagan declares National Code Talkers Day.

1984   Juan Pujol Garcia receives MBE (Member of the Order of the British Empire) award in a public ceremony.

OCTOBER 10, 1988   Juan Pujol Garcia dies in Caracas, Venezuela, after suffering a stroke.

DECEMBER 11, 1997   Eddie Chapman dies of heart failure in England.

2001   Roy Hawthorne and other Navajo code talkers are awarded Congressional Gold and Silver Medals.

NOVEMBER 8, 2012   Statue of Noor Inayat Khan is unveiled in London.

JUNE 4, 2014   Chester Nez, the last of the original twenty-nine Navajo code talkers, passes away.

APRIL 21, 2018   Roy Hawthorne dies in Arizona at the age of 92.

SOURCE NOTES

CHAPTER ONE / Juan Pujol Garcia: Storyteller Spy

p. 8. "the 'appointed scribes' . . . be found quickly." Talty, 73–74.

p. 9. "I am certain . . . they are beaten." Macintyre, (*Agent Zigzag*) 264.

p. 10. "I have observed . . . and also on Sundays." [This and all other writing samples from Garcia to the Abwehr from the National Archives UK]

p. 11. "I said farewell to the Swiss." National Archives UK, KV 2/63.

p. 13. "lack of infantry . . . defeat in Normandy." Hesketh, xix.

p. 13. "a decisive mistake . . . Pas de Calais." Holt, 589.

All other quotes from Garcia and West, pp. 10, 13–14, 16, 142.

CHAPTER TWO / Jasper Maskelyne: Magician Spy

p. 15. "I went to my doctor . . . cut my tonsils out." Grossman, film.

p. 16. "He had this . . . art of camouflage." Grossman, film.

p. 17. "If I could . . . away or more." Grossman, film.

p. 18. "We stand behind every camel." Fisher, 82.

p. 19. "I've invented . . . rescue the crew." Document 13714, Imperial War Museums.

p. 25. "You must conceal . . . bloody well got to." Fisher, 369.

CHAPTER THREE / Josephine Baker: Dancing Spy

p. 27. "He was adorable . . . black velvet dress." Baker and Bouillon, 57.

p. 31. "in constant motion . . . sounds we know." Baker and Bouillon, 55.

p. 33. "*C'est une . . . courageuse!*" Haney, 217.

p. 33. "France made me . . . as you wish." Caravantes, 84.

p. 33. "the perfect . . . *my* war." Baker and Bouillon, 19.

p. 34. "if she ever . . . to enemy capture." Schroeder, 70–71.

p. 34. "The vast chateau . . . my Belgian friends." Baker and Bouillon, 119.

p. 35. "Being Josephine Baker . . . a safety pin." Baker and Bouillon, 125–126.

p. 35. "Besides, my encounters . . . generally meant autographs." Baker and Bouillon, 125–126.

p. 36. "It can fairly . . . 'Two Loves Have I.'" Baker and Bouillon, 120.

p. 36. "We've got to . . . war on Hitler." Josephine Baker official website.

CHAPTER FOUR / Eddie Chapman: Safecracker Spy

p. 40. "he would steal . . . hurt a soul." Macintyre (*Agent Zigzag*), 8.

p. 40. "I shall go . . . come back." Macintyre (*Agent Zigzag*), 3.

pp. 40–41. "the routine was . . . all of them." Owen, 24.

p. 41. "I would like . . . German secret service." Owen, 38.

p. 42. "What work did . . . least fifteen years." Owen, 47–48.

p. 43. "I always ended . . . he, he, ha, ha." Owen, 59.

p. 44. "If caught, I . . . Reich, was death." Owen, 67–68.

p. 48. "In our opinion . . . be an agent." Macintyre (*Agent Zigzag*), 115.

p. 49. "Well. Am with . . . Good landing. Fritz." Owen, 109.

p. 50. "look, from the air . . . to Kingdom Come." Macintyre (*Agent Zigzag*), 153.

p. 53. "I pulled the . . . spewed over England." Owen, 219–220.

p. 53. "Safe. FFFFF. Will . . . in seven days." Owen, 227.

CHAPTER FIVE / Virginia Hall: Most-Wanted Spy

p. 62. "Cuthbert is being . . . have him eliminated." Pearson, 153.

p. 64. "I received a . . . have had weapons." Bohny, interview.

p. 66. "It was dangerous . . . landed, taking everything." Nallet, interview.

CHAPTER SIX / Noor Inayat Khan: Sufi Princess Spy

p. 69. "*Liberté!*" Fuller, 257.

p. 70. "She lived in . . . and beneficent beings." Khan, interview.

p. 70. "There was something . . . expected to use." Fuller, 91.

p. 70. Do you like . . . in the garden. Fuller, 37.

p. 71. What do you . . . to the end. Fuller, 42.

p. 77. "Well, you can . . . the little bulbs." Fuller, 172.

p. 81. "Cheer up . . . out of here." Fuller, 227.

pp. 82–83. "There are three . . . I am leaving." Fuller, 246–7.

p. 84. "surrounded . . . 'I'm free,' she said." Fuller, 253.

p. 84. "He had dreamed . . . she is dead.'" Fuller, 253.

CHAPTER SEVEN / Roy Hawthorne: Navajo Code Talker Hero

p. 86. "as was with all Navajo . . . lifeblood of the Navajo family." This and all other quotations, except those noted below, from author's personal interview with Roy Hawthorne.

p. 89. "Begin withdrawal at . . . to your headquarters." McClain, 26, 35.

p. 94. "took part in . . . had code talkers." Nez, 214.

pp. 95–96. "*Than-zie tlo-chin* . . . secure. Over." McClain, 199–200.

CHAPTER EIGHT / Moe Berg: Major-League Spy

p. 98. "Can any   fellows catch?" Berger, online article.

p. 98. "was an excellent . . . swiftest base runners." Berger, online article.

p. 99. "the brainiest man in baseball." CIA website.

p. 101. "He was a . . . any of them." Sherman, video.

p. 103. "the most famous . . . in baseball." Dawidoff, 72.

p. 103. "Moe was really . . . sure sounded good." Francis, online article.

p. 103. "If you teach . . . would learn baseball." Sherman, video.

p. 104. "Baseball is all . . . in their crotch." Fretts, *New York Times* article.

p. 104. "Baseball is a . . . as a spy." Fretts, *New York Times* article.

p. 105. "He'd been drilled . . . been no escape." Powers, 393.

p. 106. "Nazi" . . . "sinister eyes" Powers, 392.

p. 106. "when a runner . . . lose the war." Fretts, *New York Times* article.

p. 107. "Maybe I'm not . . . than he did." CIA website.

p. 107. "How did the Mets do today?" Anderson, *New York Times* article

CHAPTER NINE / More Surprising Spies and Unexpected Heroes

pp. 108–109. "Mr. Shaw . . . back to work soon." FBI website.

p. 110. "The indictment to . . . $10,000 fine." FBI website.

p. 112. "Fleming was . . . by gadgets." Stevenson, *A Man Called Intrepid*, 270.

p. 114. "Julia was self-admittedly . . . refuse to eat." CIA website.

CHAPTER TEN / Tools of the Trade: Secret Messages and Codes

pp. 122–123. "AWOL-LA-CHEE . . . BESH-DO-TLIZ (zinc)." McClain, 268–9.

SELECTED BIBLIOGRAPHY

BOOKS

Aaseng, Nathan. *Navajo Code Talkers*. New York: Walker, 1992.

Abtey, Jacques. *La Guerre Secrète de Josephine Baker*. Paris: Editions Siboney, 1948.

Atwood, Kathryn J. *Women Heroes of World War II: 26 Stories of Espionage, Sabotage, Resistance, and Rescue*. Chicago: Chicago Review Press, 2011.

Baker, Jean-Claude, and Chris Chase. *Josephine: The Hungry Heart*. New York: Random House, 1993.

Baker, Josephine, and Jo Bouillon. *Josephine*. New York: Paragon House, 1977.

Barkas, Geoffrey. *The Camouflage Story*. London: Cassell, 1952.

Basu, Shrabani. *Spy Princess: The Life of Noor Inayat Khan*. New Lebanon, NY: Omega, 2007.

Binney, Marcus. *The Women Who Lived for Danger: Behind Enemy Lines During World War II*. New York: William Morrow, 2003.

Breuer, William B. *Bizarre Tales from World War II*. New York: Castle Books, 2005.

Brown, Anthony Cave. *Bodyguard of Lies*. New York: Harper & Row, 1975.

Bruchac, Joseph. *Code Talker: A Novel About the Navajo Marines of World War Two*. New York: Speak, 2005.

Bull, Stephen. *The Secret Agent's Pocket Manual 1939-1945*. London: Conway, 2009.

Caravantes, Peggy. *The Many Faces of Josephine Baker: Dancer, Singer, Activist, Spy*. Chicago: Chicago Review Press, 2015.

Cheng, Anne Anlin. *Second Skin: Josephine Baker and the Modern Surface*. New York: Oxford University Press, 2011.

Conant, Jennet. *The Irregulars: Roald Dahl and the British Spy Ring in Wartime Washington*. New York: Simon & Schuster, 2008.

Dawidoff, Nicholas. *The Catcher Was a Spy*. New York: Vintage Books, 1995.

DeSaix, Deborah Durland, and Karen Gray Ruelle. *Hidden on the Mountain: Stories of Children Sheltered from the Nazis in Le Chambon*. New York: Holiday House, 2007.

Fisher, David. *The War Magician*. London: Corgi Books, 1985.

Fuller, Jean Overton. *Noor-un-nisa Inayat Khan*. London: East-West, 1988.

Garcia, Juan Pujol, and Nigel West. *Operation Garbo: The Personal Story of the Most Successful Spy of World War II*. London: Biteback, 2011.

Guterl, Matthew Pratt. *Josephine Baker and the Rainbow Tribe*. Cambridge, MA: Belknap Press of Harvard University Press, 2014.

Halberstam, Gaby. *Noor Inayat Khan*. London: A&C Black, 2013.

Haney, Lynn. *Naked at the Feast: A Biography of Josephine Baker*. New York: Dodd Mead, 1981.

Heselton, Philip. *Doreen Valiente: Witch*. Doreen Valiente Foundation / Centre for Pagan Studies, 2016.

Hesketh, Roger. *Fortitude: The D-Day Deception Campaign*. Woodstock, NY: Overlook, 2000.

Holt, Thaddeus. *The Deceivers: Allied Military Deception in the Second World War*. London: Phoenix, 2005.

Jules-Rosette, Bennetta. *Josephine Baker in Art and Life: The Icon and the Image*. Urbana: University of Illinois Press, 2007.

Khan, Noor Inayat. *Twenty Jataka Tales*. Rochester, VT: Inner Traditions International, 1975.

Macintyre, Ben. *Agent Zigzag*. New York: Broadway, 2007.

———. *Double Cross: The True Story of the D-Day Spies*. New York: Broadway, 2012.

———. *A Spy Among Friends: Kim Philby and the Great Betrayal*. New York: Crown, 2014.

McAuliffe, Mary. *When Paris Sizzled: The 1920s Paris of Hemingway, Chanel, Cocteau, Cole Porter, Josephine Baker, and Their Friends*. Lanham, MD: Rowman & Littlefield, 2016.

McClain, Sally. *Navajo Weapon: The Navajo Code Talkers*. Tucson, AZ: Rio Nuevo, 2001.

Melton, H. Keith. *Ultimate Spy: The Insider's Guide to the World's Most Dangerous Profession.* New York: DK, 2002.

Melton, H. Keith, and Robert Wallace. *The Official C.I.A. Manual of Trickery and Deception.* New York: Harper, 2010.

——. *Spy Sites of New York City.* Bellevue, WA: Foreign Excellent Trenchcoat Society, 2012.

Montagu, Ewen. *The Man Who Never Was: World War II's Boldest Counterintelligence Operation.* Annapolis, MD: Naval Institute Press, 1953.

Muller, Catel, and José-Louis Bocquet. *Josephine Baker.* London: SelfMadeHero, 2017.

National Archives UK. *Special Operations Executive Manual: How To Be an Agent in Occupied Europe.* London: William Collins, 2014.

Nez, Chester. *Code Talker.* New York: Berkley Books, 2011.

O'Donnell, Patrick K. *Operatives, Spies, and Saboteurs: The Unknown Story of the Men and Women of WWII's OSS.* New York: Free Press, 2004.

Owen, Frank. *The Eddie Chapman Story.* New York: Julian Messner, 1954.

Pearson, Judith L. *The Wolves at the Door: The True Story of America's Greatest Female Spy.* Guilford, CT: Lyons Press, 2008.

Powell, Patricia Hruby, illustrated by Christian Robinson. *Josephine: The Dazzling Life of Josephine Baker.* San Francisco: Chronicle Books, 2014.

Powers, Thomas. *Heisenberg's War.* New York: Alfred A. Knopf, 1993.

Schroeder, Alan. *Josephine Baker.* New York: Chelsea House, 1991.

Sheinkin, Steve. *Bomb: The Race to Build—and Steal—the World's Most Dangerous Weapon.* New York: Roaring Brook Press, 2012.

Shiber, Etta. *Paris Underground.* New York: Charles Scribner's Sons, 1943.

Steinmeyer, Jim. *Hiding the Elephant: How Magicians Invented the Impossible and Learned to Disappear.* New York: Carroll & Graf, 2003.

Stevenson, William. *A Man Called Intrepid.* New York: Harcourt Brace Jovanovich, 1976.

————. *Spymistress: The Life of Vera Atkins, the Greatest Female Secret Agent of World War II.* New York: Arcade, 2007.

Talty, Stephan. *Agent Garbo: The Brilliant, Eccentric Secret Agent Who Tricked Hitler and Saved D-Day.* Boston: Mariner Books, 2013.

Travis, Falcon. *The Usborne Official Spy's Handbook.* London: Usborne, 2014.

Treglown, Jeremy. *Roald Dahl: A Biography.* New York: Farrar Straus & Giroux, 1994.

Wood, Ean. *The Josephine Baker Story.* London: Sanctuary, 2000.

ONLINE ARTICLES

Anderson, Dave. "Mysterious Moe Is Declassified." *The New York Times*, January 28, 1975. Accessed September 5, 2019. https://www.nytimes.com/1975/01/28/archives/mysterious-moe-is-declassified.html

Berger, Ralph. "Moe Berg." Society for American Baseball Research. Accessed August 31, 2019. https://sabr.org/bioproj/person/e1e65b3b

Francis, Bill. "Moe Berg's Life in Baseball." National Baseball Hall of Fame. Accessed August 18, 2019. https://baseballhall.org/discover/short-stops/moe-bergs-life-in-baseball.

Fretts, Bruce. "Who Was Moe Berg? A Spy, a Big League Catcher and an Enigma." *The New York Times*, June 21, 2018. Accessed August 28, 2019. https://www.nytimes.com/2018/06/21/movies/paul-rudd-the-catcher-was-a-spy.html

Zarrelli, Natalie. "The Wartime Spies Who Used Knitting as an Espionage Tool." Atlas Obscura. June 1, 2017. Accessed August 28, 2019. https://www.atlasobscura.com/articles/knitting-spies-wwi-wwii?utm_source=facebook.com&utm_medium=atlas-page&fbclid=IwAR17U0MsPqpRz7y4J5JtFW1-xNm20uYlNWD3WokMg7Mfc-yYb53qEHUe8Dc.

ONLINE RESOURCES

Baseball Reliquary (Moe Berg) http://www.baseballreliquary.org/awards/shrine-of-the-eternals/the-shrine-of-the-eternals-2000/#morris-8220moe8221-berg

CIA website (Moe Berg)
https://www.cia.gov/news-information/featured-story-archive/2013-featured-story-archive/moe-berg.html.

CIA website (shark repellent)
https://www.cia.gov/news-information/featured-story-archive/2015-featured-story-archive/shark-repellent.html

Josephine Baker official website
https://www.cmgww.com/stars/baker/

FBI website (Velvalee Dickinson)
https://www.fbi.gov/history/famous-cases/velvalee-dickinson-the-doll-woman

National Archives UK official website
https://www.nationalarchives.gov.uk/

National Museum of the American Indian (code talkers)
https://americanindian.si.edu/education/codetalkers/html/index.html
Yad Vashem, The World Holocaust Remembrance Center (Pierre Piton)

http://db.yadvashem.org/righteous/family.html?language=en&itemId=4016935

INTERVIEWS BY AUTHOR

Bohny, Auguste. Interviewed by Deborah Durland DeSaix and Karen Gray Ruelle. November 9, 2002. Basel, Switzerland.

Eyraud, Gabriel. Interviewed by Deborah Durland DeSaix and Karen Gray Ruelle. April 3, 2007. Le Chambon-sur-Lignon, France.

Hawthorne, Roy. Interviewed by Karen Gray Ruelle. April 29, 2016. Via Skype.

Khan, Pir Zia Inayat. Interviewed by Karen Gray Ruelle. July 4, 2016. Via Skype.

Nallet, Jean. Interviewed by Deborah Durland DeSaix and Karen Gray Ruelle. November 14, 2002. Paris, France.

Nallet, Jean, and Lise Martinon. Interviewed by Deborah Durland DeSaix and Karen Gray Ruelle. April 1, 2007. Paris, France.

Swartebroecks, Alphonse. Interviewed by Deborah Durland DeSaix and Karen Gray Ruelle April 3, 2007. Le Chambon-sur-Lignon, France.

FILM AND VIDEO

Gardner, Rob, director. *Enemy of the Reich*. Unity Productions Foundation. 2014. Film.

Grossman, Gary, director. *The War Illusionist*. History's Mysteries series (History Channel). 2001. Film.

Kempner, Aviva, director. *The Spy Behind Home Plate*. Ciesla Foundation. 2019. Film.

The Princess Spy. BBC Two Timewatch. 2006–2007. TV documentary.

Red-Horse, Valerie, director. *True Whispers: The Story of the Navajo Code Talkers*. PBS. 2002. DVD.

Roch, Edmon, director. *Garbo the Spy*. First Run Features. 2009. DVD.

Sherman, Ed. "Q/A with Pulitzer Prize Winner Ira Berkow." June 27, 2016. http://jewishbaseballmuseum.com/spotlight-story/ira-berkow/. Video.

Woo, John, director. *Windtalkers*, Lion Rock Productions. 2002. Film.

RECOMMENDED READING

BOOKS
For Younger Readers

Deary, Terry. *Horrible Histories: Woeful Second World War.* London: Scholastic, 2016.

> The Horrible Histories series calls itself "History with the nasty bits left in!" and it's the truth! The blurb on the back of this entry includes "Who made a meal out of maggots?" and "Which smelly soldiers were sniffed out by their enemies?" All the ick-factor details are there, with a sense of humor and lots of cartoon-style graphics. Includes bios of some spies.

Halberstam, Gaby. *Noor Inayat Khan.* London: A&C Black, 2013.

> The heartbreaking story of Noor Inayat Khan, part of the Real Lives series.

Melton, H. Keith. *Ultimate Spy: The Insider's Guide to the World's Most Dangerous Profession.* New York: DK, 2002.

> This big book is filled with color photos and descriptions of spies and spying, equipment, gadgets, weapons, and everything else you could possibly want to know about the world of espionage.

Panchyk, Richard. *World War II for Kids.* Chicago: Chicago Review Press, 2002.

> This history, in a large format, is a good reference book for readers who want to dip in and digest the history of the war in segments. Includes activities and lots of photos.

Powell, Patricia Hruby, illustrated by Christian Robinson. *Josephine: The Dazzling Life of Josephine Baker.* San Francisco: Chronicle Books, 2014.

> This glorious picture-book biography is written in a poetic style with lots of quotes from Josephine and bold, colorful illustrations.

Travis, Falcon. *The Usborne Official Spy's Handbook.* London: Usborne, 2014.

> Covers everything from codes and disguises to tracking and shadowing. Includes lots of activities and projects, with colorful illustrations on every page.

Wiese, Jim, and H. Keith Melton. Spy University series: *The Spy's Guide to Hiding Places; The Spy's Guide to Surveillance; The Spy's Guide to Secret Codes and Ciphers; Trainee Handbook.* New York: Scholastic, 2002–2003.

> What could be better than a whole series for wannabe spies? This one is loaded with activities and illustrations.

For Older Readers

Caravantes, Peggy. *The Many Faces of Josephine Baker: Dancer, Singer, Activist, Spy*. Chicago: Chicago Review Press, 2015.

This rich biography of Josephine Baker is part of Chicago Review Press series Women of Action.

DeSaix, Deborah Durland, and Karen Gray Ruelle. *Hidden on the Mountain: Stories of Children Sheltered from the Nazis in Le Chambon*. New York: Holiday House, 2007.

This book tells the poignant true stories of some of the children hidden in the village of Le Chambon, in south-central France, and the courageous people who helped to save them.

Khan, Noor Inayat. *Twenty Jataka Tales*. Rochester, VT: Inner Traditions International, 1975.

Noor's retelling of these Buddhist legends is lovely and reflects her character.

Sheinkin, Steve. *Bomb: The Race to Build—and Steal—the World's Most Dangerous Weapon*. New York: Roaring Brook Press, 2012.

This Newbery Honor book tells the riveting story of the development of the atomic bomb, and includes the story of Moe Berg.

WEBSITES

https://americanindian.si.edu/education/codetalkers/html/index.html

This terrific website from the Smithsonian Institution's National Museum of the American Indian has loads of information about Native Americans and includes discussion questions, lessons, and activities appropriate for students. Includes a detailed section on the Navajo code talkers.

www.spymuseum.org/education-programs/kids-families/kidspy-zone

The Spy Museum in Washington, D.C., is a great place for kids to visit. The website's KidSpy Zone has kid-friendly games and activities.

https://www.bletchleypark.org.uk/about-us

Bletchley Park's website has lots of interesting information about the code breakers who worked there during World War II.

www.codesandciphers.org.uk

Originally created by the founder and curator of the Bletchley Park Museum, this website includes a challenge for wannabe code breakers at the advanced level.

www.psywarrior.com/WWIIAlliedBanknotes.html

> Sergeant Major Herbert A. Friedman's website includes a section on "propaganda leaflets in the form of banknotes [that] were prepared and disseminated by the Allied and Axis combatants." As he explains, "Few people will fail to pick up a banknote on the ground. For this reason they have always been popular as a medium of propaganda." You can see examples of some of the many different banknotes that were used in this way, including, on the second page, a French twenty-franc banknote as described by Peter Feigl.

CIA website (Moe berg): https://www.cia.gov/news-information/featured-story-archive/2013-featured-story-archive/moe-berg.html

CIA website (shark repellent): https://www.cia.gov/news-information/featured-story-archive/2015-featured-story-archive/shark-repellent.html

Josephine Baker official website: https://www.cmgww.com/stars/baker/

PHOTO CREDITS

Translation of Navajo code message on page 123:
GOOD WORK! NAVAJO CODE IS DIFFICULT. YOU ARE A SUPER SPY!

Translation of Morse code messageon page 127:
IF YOU CAN READ THIS MESSAGE THEN YOU ARE WELL ON YOUR WAY TO BEING
A GOOD SPY!

ACKNOWLEDGMENTS

The roots of this book are in my childhood, growing up during the Cold War. I was obsessed with spy shows like *Get Smart*, *The Avengers*, *The Man from U.N.C.L.E.*, *Mission Impossible*, and *The Prisoner*. Eventually I graduated to James Bond and then John le Carré, but I still have a soft spot for those old programs.

Then I discovered the true stories behind the fiction, and they were even richer and more astonishing. Juan Pujol Garcia (Garbo), the real spy, had a much better story than Jim Wormold in Graham Greene's version of his life, *Our Man in Havana*. These were actual people, with lives, with families and friends—and so much was at stake. Despite the danger and fear, they persevered. They clearly must have had a risk-taking gene, but mostly I believe their strong moral core and sense of justice impelled them to undertake those perilous missions.

When I found the Garbo exhibit at the Spy Museum in Washington, D.C., I knew I had to tell his story. And I wanted to learn more. This book is just the beginning!

I'd like to thank the many people who helped me on this journey. They include:

My folks, Barbara and Edward Gray, for indulging my childhood TV preferences and for their help with research. My husband, Lee, for his patience, for his technical skills, and for making me dinner when I was too busy writing to remember to eat. My daughter, Nina, for her enthusiasm and feedback.

Julie Dauphinais and Doug Gray, who put me in touch with Katie Franquist, who put me in touch with Navajo code talker Roy Hawthorne.

Regan Hawthorne, Paul Silverman, Robert Wallace, H. Keith Melton, Michael Wolfe, Pir Zia Inayat Khan, David Harper, the late Annik Flaud, Jean Nallet, Lise Martinon, Alphonse Swartebroecks, Gabriel Eyraud, Deborah Durland DeSaix, Sally Holmes Holtze, Ronald Blumer, Sergeant Major Herbert A. Friedman, Anne-Louise Wirgman at the Nekbakht Foundation, Ashley Mortimer at the Doreen Valiente Foundation, and the very helpful staff at the Imperial War Museums and National Archives in the UK.

And finally Maryann Macdonald and Jill Pratzon, my writing-group pals, critics, and supporters. Thank you for helping me to shape this book and for encouraging me along the way.

Thank you, all!

INDEX

Page numbers in *italics* refer to illustrations.

F

Farouk, King, 21–22
Faye, Léon, 81
FBI (Federal Bureau of Investigation), 61, 109
Feigl, Peter, 117–18, *118*
fire-resistant paste, *19,* 20
"fist" of radio operator, 43
Fleming, Ian, 112–13, *113,* 116
forged documents, 3, 20, 28, 61, 117
Free French Forces, 29, 32–37
Fuller, Jean Overton, 70, 83, 131
Funkspiel, 79–80

G

Garcia, Juan Pujol, 1–14, *7, 11,* 54, 119, 129–32
gelignite, 39, 51
George Cross, 84, 131
German code breakers, 79–80
German spies, *see* Abwehr
Gestapo, 62, 74, 76–81, 83
Goillot, Paul, 67–68
Graumann, Doctor, 42–43, 45, 53

H

Hall, Virginia, 58–68, *61, 68,* 129–32
Hawthorne, Roy, 85–97, *86, 88, 97,* 130, 132
Heisenberg, Werner, 105–6, 130
Hirohito, Emperor, viii, *x,* 87
Hitler, Adolf, vii–viii, *viii,* 2, 9, *43,* 128–29, 131
Holocaust, ix

I

invisible ink, 3–4, 33, 35–36, *36,* 44, 48, 119–20
Iron Cross, 13, 51, 130
Iwo Jima, *94,* 95–96, 131

J

Japanese code breakers, 85, 88, 92
Japanese spies, 109–10
Jersey, 40–41, 128–29
Johnston, Philip, 89

K

Khan, Hazrat Inayat, *71*
Khan, Noor Inayat, *ii,* 43, 69–84, *71, 73, 75, 84,* 104, 129–32
Khan, Pir Zia Inayat, 70
Khan, Vilayat, 73, *73,* 83

L

Lebrat, Edmond, 66, *68*
Le Chambon-sur-Lignon, *59,* 63, *63–65,* 66, *67,* 117, *117*
Légion d'Honneur, 37–38, 131
Lewin, Ben, 104
Lion, Jean, 32, 128

M

Maclean, Donald, 111–12
Majola, Paul, 117, *117*
Maquis, 58–59, *59,* 64–65, *65,* 67, *67*
Marceau, Marcel, 115
Maskelyne, Jasper, 15–26, *16, 19,* 50, 129–30, 132
Masterman, John, 49
Médaille de la Résistance, 37, 131
Medal of Freedom, 106–7, 131
MI5, MI6, MI9, as branches of British Directorate of Military Intelligence, 7, 20
Michael, Glyndwr, *116,* 116–17
Mincemeat, Operation, 113, 115–17, *116*
Montagu, Ewen, 116
Montgomery, General, 25
Morse code, 43, 72–74, 90, 120, 124–27
Mosquito, de Havilland, 44, *50*
Mussolini, Benito, viii, *viii,* 131

N

Nacht und Nebel, 81–82
Navajo ceremonies, 87–88, 96–97
Navajo code talkers, 85, 89–97, *92–93, 97,* 121–23, 129, 131–32
Nazi party, vii, *2*
nuclear bombs, 104–6